DEATH ON THE ISLES OF SCILLY
The grave in California Field

Tom Menheniott at Holy Vale on St. Mary's

DEATH ON THE ISLES OF SCILLY

The Grave in California

John Purchas

*The Sensational Story of the
Menheniott Murder Case*

DEDICATION

This book is dedicated to Tom,
Dodo, Ethel, Baldwin, Diana,
Simon, Kathryn and to the one
who was never known but is not
forgotten.

First Published 1986
by Dyllansow Truran.
Trewolsta, Trewirgie, Redruth, Cornwall.

Typeset by Helston Printers, 12 Wendron St., Helston, Kernow.
Printed by Penwell Ltd, Callington, Kernow.

ISBN 0 907566 79 0

FOREWORD

by

The Right Honourable Sir Francis Purchas, P.C.
One of Her Majesty's Judges in the Court of Appeal.

The story of Stephen Menheniott which John Purchas tells in this humanely written and highly readable book underlines dramatically the immense responsibilities, problems and potential for catastrophy involved in child care and family welfare. The book traces the history of the Menheniott family from the birth of Tom Menheniott in 1924, a robust and strong youth, who for reasons not disclosed spent the first 14 years of his life in the care of the Cornwall County Council. It may be that the first seeds of disaster were sown in that early period. In the 1940s Tom Menheniott was convicted of criminal neglect of two children of his marriage and was sent to prison. The members of the family with whom this book is concerned were born of an association with another woman. Stephen Menheniott and his elder sister Elizabeth were both taken into care; Elizabeth by the Cornwall County Council in 1953 and Stephen by the East Sussex County Council in 1959. Tom Menheniott was guilty of ill-treating both of those children. Thereafter the concatination of events unfold a drama which moves forward to the murder of Stephen Menheniott by his father; his subsequent burial in the presence of his elder sister at dead of night and the trial of Tom Menheniott at the Bodmin Crown Court in May 1977 with the inevitability of a Greek tragedy.

The decisions which exposed Stephen to the fatal brutality of his father came to be taken at a time when the responsible authorities were themselves experiencing administrative disruption and change. Acting upon the Seebohm Report Parliament had enacted the Local Authorities Social Services Act 1970. The large, monolithic Social Services Departments which came into existence as a result were, during the critical periods of Stephen's saga, creaking into motion like bureaucratic juggernauts. Stephen's was only one of a number of tragedies which occurred during this period which could at least in part be attributed to lack of experience and expertise on the part of senior welfare workers and lack of supervision of junior members of these departments. Somewhere in this reorganisation sight seems to have been lost of the following extract from paragraph 624 of Seebohm:-

> "624. The purpose of these services is to help people
> as individuals or families. Many of these people, -
> and they are often those in the greatest need - are
> helpless, inarticulate or at odds with society.
> Generally, the public are well-disposed towards most

V

of them, but public interest by itself cannot be a
sufficient guarantee against the possibility of neglect
or maladministration...."

After reading the manuscript of John Purchas's book I was forcibly reminded of this paragraph.

The East Sussex County Council Social Services Department had the misfortune of being concerned in two cases which, because of their particular circumstances, achieved exceptional notoriety; but as the author comments, there were many similar mistakes made during this formative period of the new Social Services Departments. In the light of human frailty mistakes will continue to be made. No-one who gives the matter a moment's thought will doubt the immense difficulty and stress imposed upon those authorities as they struggled to discharge the very burdensome duties imposed upon them with, almost invariably, quite inadequate resources.

It is doubtful whether the lack of communication between the two authorities concerned which allowed Stephen's father to practice brutality upon him over a period of years will recur. How it occurred is understandable. The primary duty upon a local authority had from the earliest days been to work towards the return of a child to its parents as the initial stage. This is clearly what the East Sussex County Council were intent upon doing; but they ignored the advice of the Cornwall County Council. On their part the Cornwall County Council, although knowing more about the general background and history of the family as a whole and knowing that Stephen was to be returned to his family by the East Sussex County Council, considered that as Stephen was in the care of the East Sussex County Council, this was a matter for them and did not themselves take steps to have the care order transferred from the East Sussex County Council to themselves. The true pathos of this story is probably to be found in the answer given by Mr. Davies, counsel who appeared for the East Sussex County Council at Tom Menheniott's trial, to the effect that "A lot had happened since 1972 and procedures that now existed, although it was no consolation to Stephen, would have prevented such a lack of supervision occurring."

The approach to the sensational trial which took place in the Crown Court at Bodmin during December 1977, and the trial itself with the drama and tensions involved, receive the most skilled and attractive treatment, which has only been made possible as a result of a considerable amount of research on the part of the author.

In closing and commending this book to the reader, I wish to recall stanza 77 of the Rubaiyat of Omar Khayyam which should be ever present in the minds of those concerned with the difficult and important matters of family and child welfare:-

VI

"The moving finger writes: and having writ
Moves on: nor all thy piety nor wit
Shall lure it back to cancel half a line,
Nor all thy tears wash out a word of it."

PREFACE

Imagine the idyllic Isles of Scilly in summer, twenty-eight miles south-west of Land's End. Crystal clear seas and lovely white sandy beaches. Serviced by helicopter and boat from Penzance, they are a holidaymakers dream.

Contrast this with the islands in winter: storm-bound, windswept and desolate. At such a time in early January, 1976 Stephen Menheniott, a simple and slow-witted 18 year old, until recently in the care of East Sussex County Council and returned to the Islands in 1972 against the express advice of the Cornish Authorities, met his death at the hand of his father. The long saga of ill-treatment and violence ended that January night when his father, Tom Menheniott, aided by his daughter, Elizabeth, laid Stephen to rest in a shallow grave in California Field, a part of his father's daffodil farm on the island of St. Mary's.

This tragic, yet true, story of brutality by father upon son has been skilfully woven together by the author, a well-known Penzance solicitor. The tale embraces Stephen's ordeal on the farm, the courtroom drama following his father's arrest and the subsequent Official Inquiry, published by H.M.S.O., which in its Report castigated the Social Services for their failures in safeguarding the lad's welfare.

To find out how such cruelties could be exacted by father upon son, even sometimes in the presence of islanders, the author has examined the history of the family and the reader will be asked to consider the workings of a small island community unused to criminal actions and to appreciate the insularity that is borne within it. It is a dramatic tale of cruelty and official error and with many lessons to be learned.

ACKNOWLEDGMENTS

I should like to thank the Director of Public Prosecutions for releasing to me the committal papers relating to the preliminary hearing of the Menheniott case before the Isles of Scilly Justices.

Thanks are also due to the Devon and Cornwall Constabulary for allowing photographic exhibits to be reproduced, and to Mr. Frank Gibson of St. Mary's on the Isles of Scilly for giving permission for photographs of Tom and Stephen Menheniott and of Mr. Barrie Fairest to be reproduced.

I also appreciate the co-operation of Messrs. Hibbit & Sanders of East Sussex, the official court shorthand writers who covered the Menheniott trial, who willingly passed on to me a copy of their transcript which covered all the essential evidence given at the trial.

I should also like to acknowledge the Cornishman Newspaper as my source for the post-verdict comments of Mr. Justice Willis and Counsel, and the D.H.S.S. (HMSO) Report into the management of the case of Stephen Menheniott, from which background information used in this book was obtained.

And finally I should like to thank my wife, Diana, for her typing and other assistance in the preparation of the book, and for putting up with my long absences in 'the study'.

Author's Note

The Crown Court evidence quoted in the book embodies everything relevant said by the respective witnesses. Not everything said by the witnesses is quoted, since much is repetitive and, in the nature of things, much does not read well. However, the essential sense of the evidence is accurate, as are the verbatim extracts.

The house of everyone is to him as
his castle and fortress, as well
for his defence against injury and
violence, as for his repose.

Sir Edward Coke
1552-1634

CHRONOLOGY OF EVENTS

26th February 1924	Tom Menheniott born and in the care of the Cornwall County Council until 14 years of age.
The 1940's	Tom marries. Two children of the marriage who were both taken into care by the Cornwall County Council. Tom convicted of criminal neglect and serves a term of imprisonment.
1950	Tom leaves his wife and for the next 20 years lives with Elizabeth Thomas by whom he has six children.
14th July 1952	Elizabeth (Liz) Menheniott born. Her married name is Rayner.
1953	Elizabeth taken into care by the Cornwall County Council, and Tom is convicted and imprisoned for ill-treating her.
4th June 1957	Stephen Menheniott born.
29th January 1959	Stephen taken into care by East Sussex County Council.
1965	Stephen's parents move to St. Mary's, Isles of Scilly. Stephen remains in care in Sussex.
1967/68	Stephen spends three short holidays with his parents and ultimately in the summer of 1968 is allowed by East Sussex County Council to remain with them.
2nd January 1970	Isles of Scilly Magistrates commit Tom Menheniott for trial on charge of incest relating to his 13 year old daughter's pregnancy. He is acquitted of the charge, but on 24th November 1969 all his children had been returned to the mainland and Stephen, aged 12, was placed in an East Sussex County Council Home.
1970	Menheniott's common law wife, Elizabeth Thomas, separates from Tom and leaves the islands. Liz returns to her father.
August 1972	Stephen returns to his father on a permanent basis. East Sussex County Council, de facto, cease exercising any control over him. Stephen is now aged 15 years.
9th December 1974	East Sussex County Council formally discharge Stephen from their care at the age of 17½.
26th November 1975	Stephen's last dental appointment with Mr. Barrie Fairest.
7th January 1976	Stephen dies.
Night of 8th/9th January 1976	Stephen buried in California Field. Liz aids her father in the burial.

XI

7th December 1976	Liz Menheniott tells Mr. Fairest that Stephen has gone to Sussex to see his girlfriend.
24th December 1976	Police investigation into Stephen's disappearance commences.
18th May 1977	Liz Menheniott takes police officers to Stephen's grave in California Field. Later the same day, Stephen's remains are uncovered.
19th May 1977	Dr. Hunt, a Home Office pathologist, performs a post-mortem examination.
20th May 1977	Menheniott is charged with the murder of his son.
27th July 1977	Menheniott is charged with two offences of incest relating to his relationship with his daughter Liz, and is also charged with preventing a Coroner from holding an inquest.
17th August 1977	The three day Committal hearing commences on St. Mary's.
6th to 16th December 1977	Menheniott's trial at the Bodmin Crown Court.
5th September 1978	A Department of Health and Social Security Committee of Inquiry submit their Report to the Secretary of State for Social Services, later published by H.M.S.O. under the title 'Report of the Social Work Service of DHSS into certain aspects of the management of the case of Stephen Menheniott.'
5th February 1979	Court of Appeal refuse Menheniott leave to appeal against conviction.

Chapter 1

The Burial

St. Mary's, the largest of the group of islands which collectively comprise the Isles of Scilly, 28 miles south-west of Land's End, can be reached from Penzance either by boat or helicopter. There are five inhabited islands with a total population of about two thousand. St. Mary's is the largest island but even then only has a length of some three miles from north to south and a coastline of ten miles. The islands are renowned for their magnificent seascapes, the grandeur of their rocky coastline, the secluded white sandy beaches and, inland, leafy lanes and small fields bordered by granite stone walls. A favourite spot for the holidaymaker in summer on St. Mary's is the quay at Hughtown, where each morning the pleasure launches take visitors on excursions to the off-islands, the Bishop Rock lighthouse, the Western Rocks or to the seal colonies.

The islands are certainly not a place that one would associate with violence, and indeed it has been said that the last murder there occurred over 200 years ago. In the 1970's, however, violence was to re-appear. During the evening of 7th January, 1976, William Thomas Menheniott, a small-time tenant farmer and flower grower, commonly known as Tom, had a violent argument with his son Stephen, aged 18, in their cottage at Holy Vale on St. Mary's. In the light of facts that were later to come to light, it would be hard to imagine a less appropriate name.

Holy Vale is a tranquil and remote part of the island, indeed it is near enough at the centre of St. Mary's, and although Menheniott's granite cottage was in a terrace of three, the next door property was a holiday house and often empty. The one beyond that, however, was occupied by a Mr. Banfield, who was also a farmer. Set in a small valley at the end of a lane, with surrounding high trees sheltering it from the ferocious winds that hit Scilly during the winter months, the impression given was of a picturesque little cottage with white painted framed windows and a cement-washed roof. Internally, however, on that bleak winter's night it was filthy and, surprisingly, gave the impression of not having seen a woman's hand for a long time. It presented a sordid, shabby and thoroughly dirty scene - in every way equal to the bestial events which it had witnessed in the past and which were still to unfold.

Tom Menheniott was a robust, bearded and strong man. His son, on the other hand, was simple and slow. Apart from father and son, the only others living in the cottage were Menheniott's daughter Elizabeth, or Liz as she was known, then aged 23, and her two young sons. Liz had been living at Holy Vale since 1970 and Stephen since 1972.

Liz does not know what caused the argument that January evening

13

but it occurred in the narrow passageway on the ground floor of the cottage. Menheniott hit his son with a number of rabbit punches on the back and across his face. Stephen fell to the floor where he remained for some minutes with his mouth bleeding. His father left him lying there and went to his bedroom. Liz eventually helped her brother up and got him into the bath which was on the ground floor and it was then that she noticed the marks on his back. Despite the violence inflicted upon him it appears that he was able to bath and dry himself, put on pyjamas and walk upstairs unaided.

Stephen suffered from a rash on his legs which had first appeared in the summer of 1975 and which was caused through flower picking. This type of rash is quite common on the islands which are renowned for their daffodil crops, but unfortunately it causes severe irritation. After he had taken his bath, Stephen and Liz went up to their father's bedroom. It was Menheniott's custom to put powder, cotton wool and a bandage around both his son's legs to alleviate the effects of the rash. Despite the beating he had just received, Stephen allowed his father to follow the usual routine. Stephen held on to the bedroom door and in turn put out each leg to be treated. But that night according to Liz he would not, or could not, keep still. His father, no doubt annoyed by this, pulled at one of his legs causing him to fall and hit the back of his head on the bedroom wall. Neither Liz nor her father went to his aid or offered assistance. Stephen, however, managed to crawl out of the bedroom on all fours and returned to his own room. Initially, father and daughter made no effort to comfort or tend Stephen. Instead they turned on the television in Menheniott's bedroom and watched it for a while.

About ten minutes later Stephen started to moan loudly. His father shouted at him to stop and told Liz to go along and stop him making the noise. She went to his room and found him lying naked on a cold floor. This presumably surprised her, as when last seen he had been wearing his pyjamas. He was left on the floor for a further two to three hours, moaning all the time. Eventually Liz became very worried. She knew there were two doctors on the island and that one lived just across the field from the cottage. She asked her father to get a doctor but he refused. After this, Liz went in to see her brother nearly every hour but the dreadful moaning continued unabated. If she asked him a question he would only mumble and she found him impossible to understand.

At some stage Menheniott did go in to see his son and with Liz's help he managed to lift him onto the bed. Liz put some blankets over her brother and put hot water bottles against his body as he was still moaning and seemed terribly cold. However the moaning continued on into the night as did the father's shouting.

Suddenly the moaning stopped and at about 3.00 a.m. in the early morning Menheniott went to his daughter's bedroom and told her that

Stephen was dead. He told her: 'Sorry Liz, we can't have a funeral or have a doctor.' He was all too obviously worried by the marks on the boy's back and by his general condition. Menheniott told Liz that he had two choices - to bury Stephen on the farm or tip him into the sea off Deep Point to the east. As soon as Liz knew Stephen was dead she tied up his bedroom door to stop her eldest boy from going in. When the young child asked where Stephen was, Menheniott said he had gone to the mainland to see his girlfriend.

Next day Menheniott told Liz that he had decided to bury the boy. All that day, whilst his father dug the grave, Stephen lay dead in his bedroom.

Menheniott started on his gruesome task by digging in a field by a bonfire but found the ground too hard. He then moved to a marshy field known as California Field half a mile from, and nearly due south of, the cottage and here he was able to dig a shallow grave some two feet deep.

At midnight on that cold January night it was time for father and daughter to move the body. Liz helped her father carry Stephen and together they put him in the boot of the car and drove along a rough farm track to the flower packing shed. There the body was taken out of the car, was wrapped in a tarpaulin and placed on a large hand-made wooden wheelbarrow which had a base of slatted wood but no sides.

From there, Stephen's body was trundled the two hundred yards or so across fields to the grave in California Field. Liz held a torch whilst her father placed the body in the grave, removed the tarpaulin and filled the grave with earth. Then Menheniott, with the aid of a tractor and buckrake, covered the grave with part of a tree in order to stop anyone seeing it from the nature trail which passed within about three hundred feet of the grave at the bottom of the field.

Father and daughter then retraced their steps and went to bed. Menheniott's thoughts, no doubt, were consumed by his desire for the body never to be discovered. Liz, who for a long time had been very heavily under the influence and control of her father, had very mixed emotions and it can safely be assumed that neither slept well that night.

If anyone asked about Stephen, Menheniott told his daughter to say that he had gone to Sussex to see his girlfriend. It seems that apart from this remark, Menheniott and Liz did not discuss Stephen again although it is likely that he was rarely out of their thoughts. Later on, Liz planted some bulbs on top of the grave.

In December 1976 Menheniott thought that he would have to leave Holy Vale as his landlord, Mr. Gibson, had died, and he told Liz he would have to move the body, as whoever took over the farm might find it. This macabre suggestion was forestalled by the commencement of police enquiries which started at about the same time. It was, in fact, Liz who eventually told the police about the grave and showed them where Stephen

15

lay. The grave's grisly secret was soon to be revealed.

This short version of Stephen's last hours merely serves to highlight the lengthy ordeal that he had to bear for years prior to his death. His death was to have far-reaching consequences and one is entitled to ask how such cruelties could be exacted by father upon son in a small island community without anyone approaching the authorities until after death had supervened? To answer that question, and to look at the full horrors of the case and its repercussions, it is necessary to look back at the history of the family so as to appreciate the difficulties and traumas that it almost inevitably had to undergo. It is also necessary, however, to understand the workings of a small island community unused to criminal actions of such magnitude and to appreciate the insularity that is borne within it.

Chapter 2

The Family History

Tom Menheniott's father was blind and his mother died when he was three months old and it became necessary for the Cornwall County Council to take Tom and his brother, George, into care in the mid-1920's. The Council placed them in a boys' home run by the Public Assistance Committee. Life there was not pleasant and corporal punishment was commonplace. George, in fact, ran away from this establishment when he was fourteen and had no further contact with his brother for some twenty-five years. Tom also ran away at fourteen and, like George, eventually joined the Army.

In the 1940's, Tom married and there were two children of that union, a son who was taken into care by Cornwall County Council and who died of muscular dystrophy at the age of 17, and a daughter who was also taken into care. Tom was convicted of criminally neglecting that daughter and served a term of imprisonment.

In 1950 Tom left his wife and for the next twenty years lived with Elizabeth Thomas by whom he had six children. A son was born in 1950 and Liz was born on 14th July 1952. In 1953 these two children were both taken into care by Cornwall County Council. Mrs. Thomas was by then known as Mrs. Menheniott and Tom was convicted and imprisoned for ill-treating these children. Liz was placed with foster parents in Cornwall and when they moved to Essex she went with them.

Upon release from prison, Mr. and Mrs. Menheniott lived in unsatisfactory accommodation, moving frequently, and it was almost inevitable that when another son was born in Kent in 1955 that he, too, would be taken into care by the Kent authorities, this time due to the Menheniott's lack of suitable accommodation. It is also known that at about this time Tom assaulted an N.S.P.C.C. Inspector who was taking an interest in the family.

The Menheniott's next child was a daughter born in 1956, and a year later, on 4th June 1957, Stephen Richard Menheniott was born in a small hospital, which nestled below the Common, at Redhill in Surrey. Although he was the fifth of his mother's six children by Menheniott, he was in fact her eleventh child. He weighed in at 5lbs. 4oz. and in the early weeks of his life he was never healthy and was admitted to hospital three times within six months of birth. He also suffered from a deformed palate.

The family became homeless in January 1958 and Stephen was sent to Wells House residential nursery at Epsom in Surrey, a local County Council Home. However he returned home in August 1958, as his parents had found a house to live in at Hailsham in East Sussex but, according to an N.S.P.C.C. Inspector, the home conditions were deplorable.

During 1958 Stephen went into hospital on at least two occasions. His main problem was that he had continual feeding difficulties with persistent vomiting and was suffering from lose of weight. He was referred first of all as an in-patient to Great Ormond Street Hospital. The investigations to be carried out there would no doubt have been of immense help to the boy, but unfortunately his father discharged him after two days. Later the same year Stephen was again in hospital, this time at the Princess Alice Hospital, Eastbourne, but once more was discharged at his father's behest. A little later on, in 1959 through to 1961, whilst Stephen was living with foster parents, near Handcross in Sussex, his vomiting reached the stage where he was vomiting at every meal and was losing weight fast. However he gradually grew out of this condition.

So far as Stephen's general welfare was concerned, matters were coming to a head at the time of his Eastbourne hospitalisation and on 29th January 1959 he was taken into care by East Sussex County Council and placed in a residential nursery. He was only nineteen months old but was to remain in care and with parental rights and duties vested in the East Sussex authorities until he was $17\frac{1}{2}$ years old.

As Stephen was illegitimate, the care notice was only served on Mrs. Menheniott. Tom Menheniott had no legal rights as to custody.

In December 1959, when Stephen was $2\frac{1}{2}$, he was fostered out to a young couple in their twenties. They had no children and hoped to adopt one in due time but were told that there was no question of this in Stephen's case. Later, the couple received a baby girl into their care with a view to adoption, and Stephen and the baby got on well and played with each other as normal children do.

In November 1960, Stephen's Uncle George, who was living in Hampshire, made enquiries after his brother Tom, and through those enquiries he learned of Stephen's existence. He was told that he was in care and that he had settled down well with foster parents. Uncle George showed interest in his nephew but was given no encouragement by the authorities to form a relationship with him. Unfortunately for Stephen, within a year of his Uncle's enquiries, the foster mother became pregnant and gave birth to a child. In the changed circumstances, she felt unable to cope with Stephen's demands and he was admitted to Horsgate Residential Nursery at Buckfield in Sussex. Because of his retarded development and disturbed behaviour fostering was never tried again. There was, however, a poignant moment soon after Stephen's arrival at the nursery when by chance he met his foster parents in the street and tried to get into their car.

There are in the country many people, often single, who one hears little about but who do a great deal of good - with official approval - by befriending children in Stephen's position. So it was that in early 1962 an 'aunty' was introduced to Stephen and she used to visit him at the nursery, and sometimes he would spend weekends at her house. During the same year, Mr. and Mrs. Menheniott had moved into a cottage in East Sussex.

In February 1964, Stephen left the Nursery for a Childrens' Home, Glebe House, Rotten Row at Lewes, which was near to the special school which he was to attend, but his 'aunty' kept in touch with him and visits continued.

The Childrens' Home was not far from where the Menheniotts were living and in May 1964 the Child Care Officer responsible for Stephen's welfare called on them. This was not an easy visit, particularly when the officer talked of the possibility of Stephen only having a gradual re-introduction to his parents and that the care order would remain effective, with the result that parental rights would remain vested in the East Sussex authorities. To Tom Menheniott, no doubt, this sounded like bureaucratic red tape and he 'blew a gasket' with the result that no meeting between parents and child took place.

Stephen, with an I.Q. of 89, was too bright for the special school and in January, 1966 he was transferred to the local primary school, and joined the 'slow learners' class. He remained at this school, and at the same children's home until July, 1968, when he was eleven years old. During this period of his life the feeling of those who had contact with him was that Stephen was a boy who liked to please and be helpful, but who could also be extremely irritating. He was also desperately unhappy.

Meanwhile, in 1965 Stephen's parents had moved to the Isles of Scilly and from then on Tom Menheniott seems to have developed a determination to regain possession of Stephen. It is difficult to decide whether the overriding wish was to care for his son, to have Stephen living with him, and thereby have an extra pair of hands on the farm at Holy Vale, of which he was sub-tenant, or whether his determination was merely to 'get one over the authorities' whom he detested. Certain it is, however, that in April and May, 1966, Menheniott asked the Cornish authorities to help him get Stephen home on a permanent basis. In reply to the April overture, Cornwall wrote to East Sussex, and said that they had "no confidence at all in either parent's ability to handle a difficult child. Mr. Menheniott is definitely unbalanced and bitterly anti-authority." In May they wrote: "I must warn you that Mr. Menheniott is capable of some violence if roused.... if Stephen is really very demanding and mischievous I think that this point should be borne in mind." Cornwall were clearly at this stage doing all they could to dissuade East Sussex from returning Stephen to his father.

However as time passed, it appeared to the Children's Officer for Cornwall, who in 1959 had also become the Children's Officer for the Isles of Scilly, that the Menheniotts were making real efforts to create a home atmosphere, and that it would become increasingly difficult to forestall a holiday visit at least. Indeed both father and son seemed determined to achieve that goal. The view was also taken by Cornwall that the Menheniotts' eleven year-old daughter who had basically been brought up by her parents seemed "a great deal more balanced and composed than her brothers and sisters in care." Events were thus conspiring for father and son to meet, and on the 15th August, 1967 Stephen arrived at St. Mary's, for a twelve-day holiday. According to East Sussex records, Menheniott's attitude towards the social worker who travelled to the islands with Stephen was belligerent and he made it clear that "he was prepared to co-operate with us as long as we went along with the way he decided things should go."

The visit itself appears to have been a success and further visits followed at Christmas, 1967 and Easter 1968. Three other children in care were by this time living with their parents at Holy Vale on a 'home on trial' basis. No signs of ill-treatment were evident and therefore at the end of Stephen's summer holiday visit in 1968 he was allowed to remain with his parents under the supervision of the Children's Officer for Cornwall in her capacity as Children's Officer for the Isles of Scilly, although East Sussex still retained parental rights. He had just passed his eleventh birthday.

In the early days, after his return to his family, all seemed well; he appeared to be happy and he attended the local school. But in April, 1969 he was caught stealing, and in July it is recorded that Stephen seemed to be scared of his father. By November, 1969 Stephen was admitting to the Child Care Officer that he was not sure whether he was happier on the Scillies or on the Mainland.

Soon, however, events were to move rapidly to crisis pitch, because Menheniott was charged with incest relating to his thirteen-year-old daughter's pregnancy. Menheniott denied the charge through his solicitor, Mr. Bennett of Penzance. He applied for bail but the prosecution objected. The Bench refused bail and Menheniott was accordingly remanded in custody. On the 2nd January, 1970 the Isles of Scilly magistrates committed him for trial on a charge of incest on a date unknown between early January and 27th May, 1969. Perhaps it was not coincidental that between these dates Stephen's behaviour took a turn for the worse.

Not surprisingly in the circumstances, all the children had, on 24th November, 1969 been returned to the Mainland and Stephen, now aged twelve, and a brother aged fourteen, went to an observation and assessment centre at Camborne in Cornwall for about a month. There it was found that Stephen's brother had a fractured humerus, and this brother expressed a determination never to return home. Menheniott was ultimately acquitted of the charge of incest, but his daughter was immediately put into the care of the Isles of Scilly Council. One can imagine the immense impact that this case must have had on the local community and the sense of outrage that must initially have been generated by the implications of the charge.

Although the reasons are not clear, the authorities in due course decided that Stephen should travel from Cornwall to an observation and assessment centre in East Sussex, and this he did two days before Christmas, 1969. Shelley's Home at Burgess Hill near Brighton was a County Council home for children of both sexes aged between three and seventeen years old, and Stephen was to remain there until August 1972. Stephen was very upset at this development as he wished to stay with his father. The decision to remove him, however, was clearly the correct one.

The Social Services have the interest of their charges at heart and it is therefore hard to understand why they did not put Stephen's 'aunty' in touch with him again on his return to East Sussex. Surely the kindly relationship between them should have been positively encouraged, particularly after what must have been a traumatic time for the boy. In fact the Social Services made no overtures whatsoever to this good lady who knew nothing of Stephen's return to the area.

Stephen was to remain at the assessment centre until his permanent return to the Scillies. At the Centre he was bullied, became isolated from the other children, and corresponded regularly with his family. The East Sussex authorities seemed unable, despite two care conferences in March, 1970 and May, 1971, to formulate any long-term plan for Stephen's future. At the first of these discussions there seems to have been an understanding that Stephen would never return to the Scillies. At the second, perhaps because by then Stephen had made his own preferences clear, as had his father, the East Sussex authorities' attitude became less clear, and it was from this time on that the views of East Sussex and Cornwall began to diverge dramatically.

The official report following the second case conference stated:
"Mr. Menheniott is asking for Stephen to go home
which consolidates Stephen's own wishes. The
final decision on Stephen's placement must rest
on discussions about the family between Cornwall
and East Sussex. Initial planning would seem to
necessitate the Social Worker visiting Cornwall
as soon as possible to investigate the possibility
of a holiday at home."

Almost as a repost to this, the Children's Officer for Cornwall wrote to East Sussex on the 9th June, 1971 recommending that there should be no further contact between father and son, and she said that Menheniott had beaten up an older son who had thereupon run away from home. A month later East Sussex received a letter from the Clerk of the Council of the Isles of Scilly, in which he endorsed what the Children's Officer had said and added that if Stephen should return home for a holiday "it would be difficult to keep any check on what is happening as Mr. Menheniott is a very belligerent person."

21

It was at about this time that Liz, Stephen's oldest sister, who was living in the family cottage at Holy Vale, put in two requests for him to return home for a holiday. East Sussex agreed, notified Cornwall and Stephen returned to the islands from the 24th December, 1971 to the 5th January, 1972 and appears to have enjoyed his stay. The islands, after the regimented life at the assessment centre, must indeed have seemed an idyllic place in which to spend Christmas and the New Year.

On 23rd February, 1972 the East Sussex Authorities again reviewed Stephen's case, and concluded:

"Stephen needs to be weaned from being in care. He should stay in the long-term group at the assessment centre and should be prepared for employment from there. The reasons for not allowing him to return home should be discussed at length and in depth with him by residential workers. Holidays at home (not exceeding two weeks) could be arranged. The situation should be reviewed again in October, 1972."

In April, 1972, following further requests from his father and sister, Stephen's Social Worker began planning a summer holiday visit to the Isles of Scilly commencing sometime during the week beginning 7th August. The Cornish authorities, however, seemed to have gained the clear impression that this was not to be a holiday visit but rather a permanent return to the Islands, and a flurry of correspondence was generated.

On the 7th August, 1972 the Children's Officer for Cornwall wrote a letter marked 'Personal' to the Director of Social Services for East Sussex. This letter said that news had reached her indirectly that Stephen was to be allowed to return home to live with his father. It continued:

"I feel that I should put on record my reservations as to the wisdom of such a move" and ended "I strongly deprecate any plan to return Stephen to his father, and it seems unlikely that his mother would be of any help to him. I am afraid that it would not be possible for this Department to arrange supervision if Stephen did return to the Isles of Scilly."

With this letter the Children's Officer enclosed a copy of her previous letter of 9th June, 1971, to the social worker, which also opposed Stephen's return home.

The Director of Social Services for East Sussex replied on 21st August. He said that he accepted Cornwall's reservations about Mr. Menheniott, but went on to say:

"It is also true to say, however, that we do not entirely share them, not so much in terms of the

22

nature of your feelings, but we do not share them to the same extent.... there has been a continuing and careful review of Stephen's needs by the Social Worker responsible for supervising him and the Area Director. He has also discussed Stephen with me; this review has led us to the conclusion that Stephen may best be helped by returning home. It is felt that he has a very real need to return and that we would be able to offer him a very poor emotional framework if he remained in this area. I am aware of the dangers that are embarked upon by taking such a course; I hope it will have a successful outcome for Stephen."

On 23rd August, 1972 Stephen's social worker wrote to the Clerk of the Council of the Isles of Scilly stating that Stephen, who was by then living at Holy Vale, would be remaining at home on St. Mary's and adding: "it is appreciated that the prospect of this boy being offered supervision, or the family being willing to accept it, is not feasible, but if anything should come to your notice causing you particular concern I know you will not hesitate to let us know."

Various points at this stage defy the imagination. At the age of fifteen Stephen was to be allowed to stay at home on a permanent basis despite the realisation that the home environment was unsatisfactory, that supervision was not feasible and that the Cornish authorities were totally opposed to such a move. Moreover, the decision to change what was planned as a holiday visit into a permanent home-coming seems to have been a casual decision taken either just before Stephen's return to the Scillies or, more probably, whilst he was actually there, and one that seems only to have been initiated following Cornwall's letter of 7th August. This is backed up by the views of the staff at the observation and assessment centre in East Sussex who, when Stephen went to the Isles of Scilly that August, believed, in accordance with the February 1972 case review, that he was only going for a holiday and that he would be returning to them at its conclusion.

After Stephen returned home, no-one from East Sussex visited him: East Sussex made no formal enquiries about him either of Cornwall or the Isles of Scilly authorities, nor were there any communications of any sort between the respective authorities! East Sussex had washed their hands of Stephen. They had obviously decided, one way or another, that his best interests would be served by returning him home and it was no doubt with some relief that they closed their file on 9th December 1974 with the note: "Stephen is now settled with his family in the Isles of Scilly - case closed, therefore discharged from care." He was then $17\frac{1}{2}$ years old, but effectively he had been discharged from care at the age of 15 when he returned to his family in 1972.

When East Sussex closed their file, Tom Menheniott, Liz and her first child were living at Holy Vale. Stephen's mother had already separated from Menheniott and was living on the mainland and never returned. Liz, in the next three years was to bear two more children. The sexual aspects and overtones at Holy Vale were not to be given a formal airing until the day of a meeting between the police and Menheniott at Liskeard Police Station on 27th July 1977.

Stephen managed to obtain a job in a supermarket on St. Mary's but was sacked after about six months owing to his deteriorating appearance and poor personal hygiene. Later, Stephen was employed by a local flower farmer, but when it was realised that he was not going to be able to hold down the job he was sacked and this was Stephen's last paid employment.

No-one received a welcome at Holy Vale and therefore visitors were few. Initially no-one was suspicious when Tom and Liz put the word around that Stephen had returned to the mainland. The best available evidence is that Stephen died on 7th January 1976. In the ensuing months, owing to the general way of life of the Menheniotts and due to the fact that Stephen rarely left the family smallholding, no-one appears to have been concerned as to his whereabouts. The sole exception was Barrie Fairest, a dental surgeon on St. Mary's who, at the time of Stephen's death, had been in practice on the islands for 17 years. Stephen had been his patient since November 1974 and had consulted him as late as 26th November 1975.

In fact, Fairest saw Stephen at his surgery on various occasions in October and November 1975 and was clearly of the opinion that the boy was suffering violence and he became exceedingly concerned. Fairest was, however, in considerable difficulty in bringing his fears to the attention of the authorities owing to the constraints imposed upon him by his professional position. However he was so concerned about injuries he had seen to Stephen's teeth, and as to his welfare generally, and as to the welfare of Liz's children that on or about 1st December 1975 he discussed Stephen's case with Dr. E. James, a specialist in Community Medicine, who was responsible for investigating non-accidental injuries to children. Later, on 7th December 1976, whilst treating other members of the Menheniott family, Fairest asked Liz about Stephen and she said that her father had let him go to Sussex to see his girlfriend. Those who knew the family background would, no doubt, have found that an unlikely story.

This concern over Stephen's welfare, coupled with his apparent departure from the Islands, eventually led to the commencement of police enquiries. The ensuing police interviews with Menheniott were to go unchallenged by the defence in subsequent court proceedings and can thus conveniently take their natural place in the narrative.

24

Chapter 3

The Police Investigation

On 24th December 1976, Sergeant Robinson from St. Mary's Police Station visited Tom Menheniott at Holy Vale. It was a visit which Tom must have been expecting at some stage, as Stephen's disappearance would sooner or later have to be explained. He enquired as to Stephen's whereabouts and Menheniott told him that Stephen had wanted to go to the mainland in late 1975 and set up as a scrap dealer. He said he had given permission and Stephen had left St. Mary's on the 'Scillonian' in January 1976 intending to go to his girlfriend's address in Sussex. Menheniott was unable at the time to supply the Sergeant with the girlfriend's address but about an hour later he brought a scrap of paper to the Police Station with the address 'Kathy Cole, 56 Cambridge Road, Hove, East Sussex' written on it.

The Police made further enquiries, but without result, and on 16th March 1977 Det. Supt. Lovell of Truro, accompanied by Det. Inspector Chapman and Sgt. Robinson, called on Menheniott at Holy Vale. Sgt. Robinson introduced the two officers and Det. Supt. Lovell said, "Mr. Menheniott, we have been trying to locate your son Stephen and despite all enquiries that have been made, we cannot find him. We hoped you might be able to help us."

Menheniott replied, "I can't tell you more than I told Robbie here. I am getting a bit fed up, first he came asking, then some more questioned me at Redruth and now you lot."

"I assure you," continued the Superintendent, "we are only trying our best to find your son. Would you tell us why he left home?"

"Well, he was working here with me for the old man, General Gibson. You can't check that because the old man is dead, but I will get his books to prove it."

Lovell states that Menheniott then left the car where the interview was being conducted and returned a few minutes later carrying a number of diaries and produced one for 1975 and in the back pointed out the names 'W.T. Menheniott' and 'S.R. Menheniott', supposedly written by Mr. Gibson.

According to the Superintendent, Menheniott then said, "Stephen got fed up and he said: 'Dad, I want to go travelling.' I said, 'All right, but if you make your bed you must lie on him.' He took the boat to the mainland and went to Sussex. I haven't heard from him since."

"How do you know he went to the mainland?" asked Supt. Lovell.

"I went over on the boat with him. It was the 7th January last year. I can prove what I am saying because I had an appointment with my solicitor and then the Social Security to get some money for my daughter."

"Where did Stephen get the money for his boat fare, because I understand he had been out of work for some time?"

"He had his own money, he had saved up £35, he was a careful boy."

"So you both went over on the boat to the Mainland. Now where did you leave him?"

"He got on the train. He was going to Hove, or Brighton it might have been."

"And since that day," continued Lovell, "7th January 1976, you haven't heard of him, or from him?"

"That's right, but he can look after himself. I didn't expect him to write, he wasn't very good at writing. I didn't learn to write until I was 23."

"Do you know whether Stephen informed the Department of Employment he had gone to Sussex?"

"I couldn't answer that. I don't expect so. I dropped them a note though."

"That would be from you - signed by you?"

"Yes, W.T. Menheniott."

Supt. Lovell, changing his line of questioning, said to Menheniott, "Before Stephen left he had some dental treatment to his front teeth. What caused them to be damaged?"

"Oh, he fell off some trees we were lopping. I told him not to be climbing on them, but he didn't take no notice."

"Apparently Stephen told the Dentist you had damaged his teeth."

"Now look here, I am getting a little fed up with this lot," protested Menheniott. "Stephen didn't speak very well - he was lispy, if you know what I mean - and I expect they got mixed up with what he said. I was there when he done it - t'was those trees over there," he said, pointing to some trees on a nearby hedge to the East.

"Have you any idea at all where he may have gone?"

"He had a girlfriend called Kathy Cole at Hove. He said he was going to see her."

"We have traced her and she hasn't seen him for over two years."

"Now look here, as soon as I get things squared up here I will make my own enquiries amongst the travellers. I can get 3,000 of them asking around. They can find things that you can't." So ended Supt. Lovell's first encounter with Menheniott.

The next meeting between them was a chance one in the main street of St. Mary's the following morning. The Superintendent said, "Yesterday you told us that you and Stephen went to the Mainland on the boat on 7th January. Are you sure that was the date?"

"Yes," Menheniott answered. "I told you I had to see my Solicitor on the 7th. We went over that day, but now thinking about it, it might have been the day before - the 6th. It was the 6th or 7th, I know that."

"I know you told us Stephen had not written to you since he left. Could he have written to your daughters?"

"No, I know that because any letters they get, I read for them. Stephen couldn't hardly write, he couldn't even spell my name."

"Aren't you a bit worried about him?"

"He can look after himself. If anything happened to him, I would soon know. The travellers would get in touch with me. I expect he's doing a bit of scrap metal up around the Sussex area."

Exactly two months were to elapse before Menheniott's next interview with the Police, and this illustrates the thoroughness with which the Constabulary were conducting their enquiries. Certainly the month of May, 1977 was to be a crucial one in the Menheniott household and so far as direct Police involvement with Tom Menheniott was concerned it got off to a start on 17th May when Sergeant Robinson and P.C. Oram called at Holy Vale at 7.15 p.m. and the Sergeant said, "We would like you to come down to the Station. You can come with us in the Land Rover."

Menheniott replied, "What's that for, mate?"

Sgt. Robinson said, "Superintendent Lovell is coming over and he wants to see you."

With that, Menheniott went ghostly white and staggered backwards. Sgt. Robinson quickly moved behind him, anticipating that he was about to collapse, but he quickly regained himself. He was then ushered into the Landrover and Sgt. Robinson said, "To be perfectly fair with you, Tom, I must now tell you that I am arresting you on suspicion of the murder of your son, Stephen. You are not obliged to say anything but anything you say will be taken down in writing and may be given in evidence."

Menheniott replied, "Yes, all right."

On the way to the Police Station Menheniott said, "I hope you've got the evidence. You're going to have to do a lot of ringing around. You've arrested me for something I know nothing about."

At the Police Station a solicitor, Mr. Phillo, was present whilst Menheniott was searched and routine documentation completed.

Next day, 18th May, Supt. Lovell and other officers went to Holy Vale and interviewed Liz, who by then had suffered a stroke. This was a vital meeting and during it Liz told the officers where the grave was, showed them the tarpaulin in which Stephen's body had been wrapped and then took them to California Field and indicated where Stephen's body lay. This was a terrible time for Liz, worried beyond measure as she was by the happenings of that January night the previous year, by the manner of Stephen's death and ill as she had by then become, and she found it almost impossible to walk to the grave and indeed had to be carried most of the way.

Later the same day Supt. Lovell was present when Dr. A.C. Hunt, a Home Office Pathologist, supervised the digging in California Field in the area indicated by Liz. Eventually a badly decomposed body was uncovered about two feet below the surface and Barrie Fairest, Stephen's Dental Surgeon, identified it, from his Dental Records, as being Stephen's body. The body was removed to St. Mary's Hospital Mortuary where the next morning Dr. Hunt performed a post-mortem examination.

At 4.10 p.m. that afternoon, after the discovery of the body, Menheniott was again interviewed at the Police Station, this time by Det. Chief Supt. Sharpe, who was accompanied by other officers. He introduced himself whereupon Menheniott asked for his solicitor to be present, and again Mr. Phillo was called and remained during the interrogation.

Det. Chief Supt. Sharpe said, "Tom, you know you are not obliged to say anything unless you wish to do so but what you say may be put into writing and given in evidence. Tom, on the 16th March this year, Mr. Lovell and Mr. Chapman here, came to see you and questioned you about the whereabouts of Stephen. You said the last time you saw Stephen was on the 7th January, 1976, when you went with him to Penzance by the 'Scillonian' and that Stephen caught the train from Penzance to look for a job."

Menheniott replied, "I won't swear to it exactly, not like that. If I recall near enough he was heading for his girlfriend."

"You said Tom, 'He had a girlfriend called Kathy Cole at Hove. He was going to see her'."

"I remember that."

"And you said after that, that that was the last time you saw Stephen and you have not heard from him since."

"Agree."

"Do you mean that you agree that is what you said?"

"Yes, that's what I said."

"And have you heard from him since that time?"

"No, not heard. No letters."

"Has he been back on the farm after that date?"

"Could have come back."

"Did Liz ever tell you he had been back?"

"No, not to my knowledge."

At this stage the interview was to take an interesting turn when Supt. Sharpe produced a letter.

Some three weeks before this interview with Menheniott, the Police had interviewed Mr. Drew, the Manager of the Penzance Unemployment Benefit Office, who had told them that Stephen had been continuously unemployed during the second half of 1975 and had last signed on at the Office on 16th December, 1975. He said that as Stephen had failed to sign

28

on again, a form of enquiry would have been sent to his home address. The enquiry form must have been returned otherwise a note would have been made on the file for the matter to be investigated, but the form had been destroyed owing to normal office procedure. However, Mr. Drew still had on his file an undated letter purporting to come from Stephen and which he believed had been stapled to the enquiry form. This was the letter which was now shown to Menheniott. It read:

S.R. Menheniott
Sussex.

"Dear Sir,
    I am stopping in Sussex to see if I can get a job for myself because there is no jobs on the Isles of Scilly for me which I can do but flowers, but the crop is bad or in other words the crop is low, so I am trying to get a job planting hops etc.

Yours faithfully,
S.R. MENHENIOTT

Please Dad Post this on to Penzance."

On being shown this letter Menheniott said, "I wrote the letter. Somebody else signed it. I wrote the letter on behalf of my boy."
    "Who signed the letter?" asked Supt. Sharpe.
    "I don't know. Come on, that was a copy. I didn't send that. I didn't write that address at the top and I didn't write that last line. That isn't my writing, or somebody has got a very good copy of my writing. I didn't write the last line."
    Supt. Sharpe said, "So are you agreeing that you wrote that bit in there, but you didn't sign it. You didn't write the address at the top and you didn't write that last line?"
    "I can't recall the letter. Stephen asked me to write it for him so he could copy it and he could send it on."
    "Are you agreeing then that that is your writing?"
    "Yes, but as I said, I didn't put the name at the top, sign it or put the last line. I put 'Sussex' at the top."
    "Why did Stephen want to send a letter like this?" asked Supt. Sharpe.
    "He was having letters from them. We got umpteen home and he wanted to tell them he was going to Sussex. I drafted it out and told him to put the address at the top."
    "Liz says that you wrote the letter and Stephen signed it at home."
    "I accept that."
    "When did you give Stephen the letter? Was it just before he went to

Sussex?" asked Supt. Lovell.

Menheniott replied, "I don't know. About a week before he went over the Mainland."

"But Liz said you wrote the letter," Supt. Sharpe said. "Stephen signed it out at Holy Vale. When I said that just now, you said you accept that. Do you mean that you accept that Stephen signed the letter or that Liz said he signed the letter?"

"I'll stick to what I said the first time."

"Now come on," said Supt. Sharpe. "What do you mean?"

"I think we will leave that one there."

"When I saw you in March," interposed Supt. Lovell, "You said that you had dropped a note to the Ministry of Labour."

"Yes," Menheniott agreed, "On one of their official forms."

"Tom, they have never received any other letter but this one," Supt. Lovell replied.

"I sent one and it had better be there, mate."

Supt. Sharpe, changing tack and going for the jugular, said, "Let's leave the letter. Tom, we have recovered Stephen's body in a shallow grave which had been dug in the bottom corner of California Field, which is part of the farm on which you work. It was in the bottom right-hand corner, where some large weeds were growing. In the field is a bean crop and the grave was discovered at the bottom, which is not cultivated. Does that surprise you?"

"Doesn't surprise me," Menheniott said flatly. "I will hold there until I am charged. Liz told you where it was?"

"Yes, she did," replied the Superintendent.

Menheniott said, "I will tell you word for word what she said. She said we were short of money and Stephen was ill and he died - and that's as far as I'm saying. I dug the grave and buried the body."

"Liz says that you went there late at night, dug a big pit."

"It was in the evening."

"Was this about March to April, or even May of last year?"

"I can't swear to it."

"Anyway, it was after the 6th January?" asked Sharpe.

"Yes, but I will stop there."

"Right," said Sharpe, "But do you admit that Stephen died, that you dug the grave and you buried the body?"

"Yes," agreed Menheniott, adding "Stephen had been ill and I had financial trouble. He died in the night. He had a bath the night before, to tell you the truth."

"You say he had been ill. What was wrong with him?"

"He had something wrong with his leg down there," said Menheniott, pointing to his right calf, "but I don't want to say anything until my proper Solicitor gets here."

30

The interview was then concluded and resumed next morning, when Menheniott's 'proper' solicitor, Mr. Jack Bennett of Penzance was present.

Supt. Sharpe reminded Menheniott that he was still under caution and reminded him also of the main points that had come out at the previous interview. Menheniott agreed that that was 'near enough' what had been said and Jack Bennett said, "That's almost word for word with what I have here in Mr. Phillo's notes." Supt. Sharpe then said to Menheniott, "I now propose to question you further concerning the circumstances leading up to Stephen's death. Elizabeth says that Stephen had a bad leg, she says you were in your bedroom watching T.V. and she called Stephen in to your bedroom for you to dress his leg. You told him to hold his leg up and then you got annoyed because he couldn't hold it up properly. You pulled his leg in a violent way, which made him fall back and he hit his head on the floor or something."

"No Sir," protested Menheniott.

"Liz also says that Stephen crawled back to his bedroom. He was moaning and groaning all night and in the morning you went in to see him. Then you told her he was dead."

"That last part's right."

"Do you mean about finding Stephen dead?" asked Sharpe.

"Yes. What I done first was consulted Liz. We agreed to leave him there. I dug a grave during the day, buried him that night."

"Liz says that you did say to her you couldn't give Stephen a proper funeral and that you had two choices. One was to throw him over 'Deep Point' and the other was to bury him on the farm."

"I did say we couldn't give him a proper funeral because of a shortage of money," agreed Menheniott.

Sharpe continued: "Liz has described how you sat on the bed and how Stephen came in to have his legs dressed. She says you got upset with him and yanked his leg in a violent way, causing him to fall over backwards and hit his head."

"No."

"A post mortem has revealed that Stephen had been the subject of some considerable violence."

"The injury he had was falling down a tree the same time as he hurt his teeth."

"When did he hurt his teeth?" asked Sharpe.

"I don't know how long ago."

"Which tree did he fall from?" asked Supt. Lovell.

"It's the one where I have got the block and tackle," replied Menheniott. "It's the one in the corner where you saw me the last time."

"When did he fall down the tree?" asked Lovell.

"About a week before he died," replied Menheniott.

31

Sharpe asked, "Do you wish to make a statement giving your account of what happened, or you can write it yourself?"

Mr. Bennett intervened, and said, "My advice must be that he does not make a statement at this stage."

At 12.20 p.m. the same day, Supt. Lovell charged Menheniott and said, "William Thomas Menheniott you are charged that you at St. Marys, Isles of Scilly between 26th December, 1975 and 19th May, 1976, did murder Stephen Richard Menheniott contrary to Common Law. Do you wish to say anything? You are not obliged to say anything unless you wish to do so but whatever you say will be taken down in writing and may be given in evidence."

On the advice of his Solicitor, Menheniott replied, 'No'.

From thereon Menheniott was remanded in custody at Exeter Prison. He attended numerous remand hearings during which time the Devon and Cornwall Constabulary, and the Director of Public Prosecutions, continued to assemble their evidence and prepare for the Committal hearing, which would take place in due course before the Isles of Scilly Justices.

There were, however, to be two further meetings between Menheniott and the Police. The first was at Liskeard Police Station on 15th June, where Menheniott had been brought following his remand appearance before the Liskeard Justices. By this time Michael McInnes, a swashbuckling young solicitor in Jack Bennett's practice, who in 1983 became a full-time magistrate in Hong Kong, had taken over the conduct of the case, and was present at this interview. Dept. Supt. Lovell was the interviewing officer and he wished to put certain allegations to Menheniott.

"Are you the father of Elizabeth Anne Rayner, nee Menheniott," he asked, "Who was born on the 14th July, 1952 at Greensplatt, St. Austell, to Mrs. Elizabeth Eileen Thomas, who was at one time living with you as your wife? Your name is recorded on her Birth Certificate as being her father."

Menheniott replied, "No answer."

Lovell continued, "I understand that Mrs. Thomas has said previously that you are not the father, but she now says that she only said that because she was frightened of you and what you would do to her if she told the truth."

Menheniott again replied, "No answer."

"She says you are definitely the father of Elizabeth and that you are well aware of this fact."

"No answer."

Lovell went on, "Elizabeth Rayner alleges that you have been having intercourse with her since she was fifteen years old, is that true?"

Again Menheniott replied, "No answer."

"Elizabeth Rayner says you have been sleeping together regularly

32

since then and that intercourse has taken place repeatedly."

Menheniott: "No answer."

The interview then ended and Menheniott was returned to the Police cells pending his return to Exeter Prison.

That interview, however, had its sequel when on 27th July Det. Supt. Lovell again saw Menheniott at Liskeard Police Station. He said, "William Thomas Menheniott, three additional charges are being preferred against you. I will read them over and I would advise you not to say anything until you have had advice from your Solicitor.

These charges are:

"That you between the 26th December, 1975 and the 31st May, 1976, at St. Mary's in the Isles of Scilly, intending to prevent the Coroner of West Cornwall from holding an Inquest in the execution of his duty upon view of the dead body of Stephen Richard Menheniott, who died a violent or an un-natural death of which the cause is unknown, did bury the said body in a field known as California Field in the Isles of Scilly, contrary to Common Law."

"That you between the 1st April, 1975 and the 31st March, 1976, at St. Mary's in the Isles of Scilly, had sexual intercourse with Elizabeth Anne Rayner whom you knew to be your daughter, contrary to Section 10(1) of the Sexual Offences Act, 1956."

"That you between the 1st and 30th April, 1976, at St. Mary's in the Isles of Scilly had sexual intercourse with Elizabeth Anne Rayner whom you knew to be your daughter, contrary to Section 10(1) of the Sexual Offences Act, 1956."

Lovell then said, "Do you wish to say anything? You are not obliged to say anything unless you wish to do so but whatever you say will be taken down in writing and may be given in evidence."

Again on legal advice, this time from Mr. Bennett, Menheniott replied, "No."

Chapter 4
The Committal Hearing

The police inquiries, and interrogations of Menheniott having now been completed, his legal advisors had to decide which counsel to instruct to advise generally on the case, and to represent Menheniott at the forthcoming Committal hearing. They chose Graham Neville, perhaps the most able criminal barrister on the Western Circuit who had Chambers in Exeter and who was later to become a Crown Court Judge.

There were two main aspects that the defence lawyers had to consider in the run-up to the committal hearing. First, should they elect for publicity? Often publicity is requested where the defence wish to contact missing witnesses and believe they can do so through the medium of the Press. Unless publicity is requested the only information the Press may publish prior to the Crown Court hearing relates to such matters as the name and address of the defendant, the charge which he faces, the name of his lawyer and such like. The second matter they had to decide was whether they should allow the committal to proceed merely by way of the prosecution handing in their witnesses' statements, or whether they should require the prosecution witnesses to give evidence in person, and thereby open themselves to cross-examination.

At an early stage, the defence solicitor made what can only be described as a tactical blunder. He elected for publicity. There was nothing to be gained by asking for reporting restrictions to be lifted - on the contrary, there was much to lose. One only has to look back to the committal hearing in 1957 of Dr. John Bodkin Adams, an Eastbourne G.P. who was charged with the murder of one of his patients, a Mrs. Morell, through the administration of drugs, to see the awful publicity that can be brought to bear upon an individual at a preliminary hearing. It is true that Dr. Adams was eventually acquitted, aided considerably as he was by his very able leading counsel, Geoffrey Lawrence, Q.C., but it is equally true that one of the direct consequences of that case was the setting up of the Tucker Committee which reported in 1958 and the ensuing, if belated, enactment of the Criminal Justice Act, 1967, which only allowed Press coverage of committal hearings if the defence specifically requested it.

As a result of the defence decision to request publicity in the Menheniott case, the Committal hearing obtained large 'banner' headlines in the Press, and one is entitled to ask what benefit accrued to Menheniott as a result of that decision? What cannot be disputed, however, is that the Defence made the correct decision in requiring certain prosecution witnesses to give evidence at the Committal hearing on St. Mary's.

So the ground rules having been laid, the scene was set for the first stage in the judicial process, the preliminary hearing, which commenced on 17th August 1977 and was to last for three days. Circumstances had dictated that the hearing took place at the height of the holiday season and the main street of Hugh Town was thronged with people. The Court House, in the Town Hall, stands in the main street about a quarter of a mile from the Quay and a mile from the Heliport and a similar distance from California Field.

Menheniott, fifty-three, well-built and bearded, travelled to St. Mary's by helicopter and was accompanied by Supt. Lovell and other officers. The Courtroom is small and was packed to capacity with witnesses, counsel, police officers and the general public. At precisely 10.00 a.m. the Chairman, Alderman W.C.T. Mumford, called the court to order and the hearing commenced.

Menheniott was now facing eight charges: of murdering Stephen, four of intending to cause him grievous bodily harm, of preventing the West Cornwall Coroner from holding an inquest by burying Stephen's body in California Field and two charges of incest relating to his relationship with Liz. After these charges had been put to Menheniott, Graham Neville, chunky, slightly pompous but highly effective, rose to his feet. He asked the court to re-impose the reporting restrictions which had been lifted in the case of the murder charge. He reminded the Bench that they had never been lifted in respect of the other charges and asked the Court to accept his view that Press reporting might be prejudicial to the Defence.

In reply, Mr. David Elfer, Counsel instructed by the Director of Public Prosecutions, said the application came too late and was misconceived. The other charges were all part of the story leading up to the murder, and the Defence had already agreed to the lifting of reporting restrictions in the most serious offence in the criminal calendar. After considering the defence application, the Bench decided not to re-impose reporting restrictions and the Press were accordingly free to report the hearing.

Mr. Elfer, in his opening speech to the Magistrates, submitted that Menheniott had done unlawful acts of violence to Stephen which had killed him. There had been assaults upon Stephen and there had been neglect to obtain medical treatment for him in respect of the assaults, and those assaults and that neglect were a substantial cause of the boy's death. "If the Defendant did them with intent to cause death that is murder. If he did them with the intention of interfering with his health, that is murder," said Mr. Elfer.

"It was a night in January of last year," he continued, "lit only by a torch held by this Defendant's daughter, Elizabeth, that this Defendant buried the body of his eighteen year-old boy. He buried him in a shallow

35

grave in the marshy corner of a field known as California Field in Holy Vale on land of which he was a sub-tenant. The reason he buried the body was because he had killed him. There were marks of recent violence on the body which the Defendant did not want anybody to enquire into. Nobody such as a doctor, a coroner, and worst of all a policeman."

Prosecuting Counsel went on to explain that Menheniott went to various lengths to ensure that the grave would not be discovered. First, he laid logs and branches over that part of the field so that it should be obscured from the prying eyes of anyone walking along the nature trail which ran at the bottom of the field. Secondly, he spread the story around that Stephen had gone to the mainland, to Sussex, to try his fortune as an itinerant scrap metal merchant and to find an old girlfriend. Furthermore, Stephen had been in receipt of unemployment benefit, and it was important that they be informed of Stephen's departure from the Islands. Menheniott, therefore, forged the letter referred to earlier, making it appear to have come from Stephen, and in which he asked his father to tell Social Security that he had gone to the mainland.

But Menheniott, said Mr. Elfer, had overlooked two things. One was the dentist on St. Mary's, Mr. Fairest, who had seen the marks of violence on the boy's face and mouth and was concerned when he did not return for treatment; the other was the conscience of his own daughter, Elizabeth, for it was she who subsequently told the police of the grave in California Field. "The frailty, slightness and slowness of this boy being the absolute antithesis of the defendant, seems to have brought out in the Defendant the true bully," he said.

It is not proposed at this stage to deal in detail with the evidence of the more important prosecution witnesses, since their evidence can more conveniently be dealt with in the Crown Court context.

The first prosecution witness to give evidence before the St. Mary's Justices was Elizabeth Anne Rayner (Liz), Menheniott's daughter. She, it will be recalled, had suffered a stroke and came into Court using a three-legged walking aid. A policeman and another Prosecution witness were sitting next to Mrs. Rayner in court and the Defence objected to this, and eventually the Court was cleared of all witnesses including Police officers.

The giving of evidence was clearly going to be a traumatic experience for Menheniott's daughter. The Clerk of the Court, Mr. Forster, warned Mrs. Rayner that she did not have to say anything that might incriminate her. In general terms, her evidence centred on her statements that her father had assaulted Stephen. "I cannot put into words," she said, "how he treated Stephen. He used to hit him. He used to hit him with his hands or anything he could get his hands on: a brush or a stick or a piece of scaffolding. He mostly hit him in temper. He hit him hard. Stephen would collapse on the floor." And then, later, she said, "I saw marks on his ears. His ears would burst and horrible stuff came out. It was yellow. That came out every time he hit him." She also said, "I found blood on Stephen's pillowcase. I found that nearly every day towards the end of Stephen's life. His teeth caused that blood." Liz also gave evidence on the immediate events leading up to Stephen's death and of his burial.

Menheniott's former common-law wife, Elizabeth Ellen Thomas of Redruth, also gave evidence. She gave background details of family life and said she finally left Holy Vale permanently in 1970. Of Menheniott's general attitude to Stephen in the earlier days, she said, "He was always on to him because he could not work as fast as the others. He would shout at Stephen and hit him. He would hit him anywhere. He hit him with his hand. As he was not so strong as the others Stephen used to cry a lot."

Under cross-examination by Mr. Neville, Mrs. Thomas vehemently insisted that Tom was Liz's father and furthermore said that if necessary she would be prepared to submit to a blood test to determine paternity. This line of cross-examination clearly had some bearing on the future defence to the two charges of incest. In the event, Mr. Elfer was later to tell the court that the Prosecution would be offering no evidence on those charges. Taking all factors into account, this was clearly a wise and humane decision.

Mr. Fairest, the St. Mary's dental surgeon, gave evidence of treatment given to Stephen, of suspicions he formed as to the causes of injuries he noticed to Stephen's face and jaw, and of assistance he gave in the removal of a badly decomposed body from the grave in California Field. He said he was unable to recognise the body from its physical features, but that he examined the body whilst it was still in the grave and from examining the teeth against his dental records he was satisfied that the body was Stephen's.

Mrs. Margaret Allwright, a year older than Stephen and the fourth child of Menheniott's liason with Mrs. Thomas, also gave evidence. She spoke of a three-month period in 1972 at Holy Vale and said that during that time her father would either hit or kick Stephen every day. "Mostly he hit him with his fists. Sometimes he would kick him, put the boot in. Then (Stephen) would roll up in agony, and go to the floor. Then Dad would just go off and leave him alone and sit down and cool off."

Mrs. Allwright, in answer to further questions from Mr. Elfer, said that she left the Islands for Redruth towards the end of 1975 and that this was the last time she saw Stephen. She did, however, return to Holy Vale on 1st March, 1976 to give her sister a hand, and Stephen was not at Holy Vale then. "I asked Dad where he was and he said he was on the Mainland with his girlfriend. I never saw Stephen after asking that."

Mrs. Allwright's husband, Adrian, told the court that in 1975 he spent six weeks at Holy Vale potato picking. He said that within ten minutes of his arrival he saw Tom hit Stephen "once, maybe twice" because something was wrong with the dinner. Mr. Allwright said that on another occasion Stephen made the tea too hot for one of the children and Tom threw it over the boy. Mr. Allwright recalled that there was yet another occasion when he walked into the dining room: "When I came into the room Mr. Menheniott was punching Stephen. He was punching him around the body. He did it more than once - two maybe three times."

Summing up, Mr. Allwright said that Tom "treated Stephen like a slave in his everyday life. He had him doing everything. He changed the babies every morning, babysitting every night and several mornings during the week. Stephen was the one who usually had to bring out the food and make the tea." At the end of the six weeks of potato picking, Mr. Allwright left the island and never saw Stephen again.

Stephen's eldest brother, William, gave evidence to the Court of beatings he witnessed during visits in the 1970's and said, "My father treated Stephen like an au pair boy. By that I mean that he used to be a lackey. He had to do the housework."

William's wife, Heather, also gave evidence on behalf of the Prosecution and mentioned one incident of importance in particular: "We visited Holy Vale on Boxing Day, 1975. On that day, one of Stephen's front teeth was missing and the other was half broken off. He had bruises on his face on the upper lip and going on to his right cheek." This was an occasion, it will be recalled, less than two weeks before the presumed date of Stephen's death, and gives a clear indication of the state of his health in those last days.

Mr. John Russell Banfield, a farmer, gave evidence next and said that he lived in Holy Vale Farmhouse which was part of the same terrace of houses as Holy Vale Cottage. Mr. Banfield said, and he seems to have been mistaken over the dates, that he last saw Stephen between April and May of 1976. He was, however, quite clear as to Stephen's condition on the last day that he saw him: "I saw him come out of his house when I was passing shortly before we were told he had gone away. As he walked across in front of me he could hardly walk at all. He was all hunched over and his arms were around his chest. He was shuffling. The right-hand side of his face was all puffed up, and I could see that a few teeth were missing."

Mr. William Richard Mumford also gave evidence, and said that he worked for Mr. Gibson, Menheniott's landlord, for about fourteen years. He said that at the beginning of 1975 he saw Menheniott treating Stephen "pretty rough, like a dog. I was planting potatoes," he said, "and Tom threw a tray right over the boy and knocked him down. Tom held the tray and dropped it down on Stephen's chest."

The next witness was a docker and part-time taxi-driver, William Henry Hall, who told the Court that Menheniott helped him to maintain his car, and that occasionally he visited Holy Vale for that purpose. On one occasion he saw Stephen come out of the cottage. His father told him to get back to work and picked up a piece of wood and hit Stephen across the

38

body with it. "On another occasion I went up with the car and Stephen had a piece of rope tied around his waist - the rope was about six to eight feet long and the other end was tied to the glasshouse. On that occasion I was up there for half an hour and Stephen was tied up for that length of time."

Hall's opinion was that "Stephen appeared to be cowed by his father, scared of him. I never heard Stephen complain or put up any form of resistance to his father."

On yet another occasion, the milkman, Mr. Perkovic, gave evidence of an assault on Stephen, and gave a graphic description of the apparent relationship between father and son. "The way I pictured Stephen was as a nervous, fragile, and small fellow. When talking to me alone he seemed to be the sort of person who wanted to converse and to be friendly, but when his father came on the scene he just changed completely; he became nervous and scared."

The first expert witness for the prosecution was Alexander Souter Davies, a Consultant Oral Surgeon and a registered dental practitioner who worked at the Plymouth General Hospital. His evidence can more conveniently be dealt with in the context of the Crown Court hearing. He did, however, cause a sensation when, in order to explain the damage to the skull and teeth, he produced Stephen's skull from a brown cardboard box.

A café proprietor from Hayle, Mr. Maggs, said he visited Menheniott at Holy Vale about three times either in late 1974 or 1975. He said Stephen had a "very hunched up, cowering appearance, rather like a frightened animal. He was very gaunt and pale, very poorly clothed and rather dirty. Over his fore arms, hands, face and neck he had what I can only describe as sores." He also said that "I couldn't understand anything which Stephen said, he tended just to mumble." Under cross-examination, Mr. Maggs said Stephen was "emaciated" in appearance and "there seemed to be quite a few of Stephen's teeth missing and they seemed to be very black."

Mrs. Frances Margaret Rosamund Hicks, a riding instructor, told the court that on one occasion in either 1975 or 1976 she was taking a group of visitors out for a ride and as she came round a corner by Mr. Banfield's house at Holy Vale she saw Menheniott standing on the path by the cottage and he was punching Stephen violently on the head. Stephen had his hands and arms up over his head and he was just cowering. She saw at least four punches land. Menheniott nodded his head at her as she rode past.

A Mr. Smith of Market Place, Penzance, said that he lived on St. Mary's from 1961 to October 1975 and knew both father and son. He described Stephen as looking "like a little dog that had been beaten all the time," and he had seen bruises on his face and arms.

The next witness to be called by the prosecution was the Home Office Pathologist, Dr. Albert Charles Hunt, and he gave detailed evidence of the injuries suffered by Stephen. He produced four fractured ribs and said that a head injury had been caused by a blow and that Stephen had lost three front teeth. He also gave evidence of supervising the removal of Stephen's body from the grave and the subsequent post-mortem.

Concerning the letter referred to earlier by Mr. Drew of the Penzance Unemployment Benefit Office, it will be recalled that Menheniott told the police that he wrote the letter on behalf of Stephen, but that someone else signed it, that he did not write the name at the top and that he did not write the last line. To rebut this, the prosecution put in a written statement from Mr. Roland Alfred Page, a Principal Scientific Officer with the West Midland Forensic Science Laboratory in Birmingham. He said his findings in relation to the letter produced were:

1. The handwriting evidence is consistent with William Thomas Menheniott being the person who wrote the name 'S.R. Menheniott' in block letters and the last sentence, "Please Dad....."

2. The handwriting evidence with regard to the signature is inconclusive; however, on the evidence available my view is that William Thomas Menheniott is more likely than Stephen Richard Menheniott to be the person who wrote it."

A written statement was also put in from Kathleen Cole of Brighton, the girl Stephen allegedly left the island to see. She said that she met Stephen at Shelley's Reception Centre at Burgess Hill in Sussex in the early 1970's. She was quite friendly with him but had not seen him since then. She had, however, received letters from him and in a letter written around Christmas 1975 he had invited her to the Isles of Scilly. She replied saying that she would love to go, but heard no more from him. A sad and short dialogue between two lonely people.

A neighbouring farmer, Billie Hicks, told the court that he last saw Stephen around Christmas, 1975. Stephen had called on him to tell him that one of his sheep was on its back. He noticed that Stephen had a large bruise at the side of one of his eyes.

This outline of the Crown's case concluded proceedings, and it only remained for Menheniott to be asked if he wished to call evidence or say anything. Menheniott, through his counsel, Graham Neville, said, "I am Not Guilty and I reserve my defence." With that, the magistrates committed Menheniott to stand trial.

So ended the preliminary hearing, a hearing which must inevitably have caused some consternation and heart-searching amongst those who had witnessed brutality by father upon son. Public attention, however, would now be focused on Bodmin, the Cornish capital and the seat of the Crown Court. There was to be a considerable delay before the trial opened, and the time was used by both the defence and the prosecution to consolidate their positions and marshal their evidence, and would allow Menheniott time to brood on the future and, possibly, the past.

Chapter 5

The Trial

DAY ONE

The trial opened at the Bodmin Crown Court before Mr. Justice Willis on Tuesday, 6th December 1977 and was to end on 16th December. Mr. David Owen-Thomas, Q.C., led for the Crown with David Elfer as his Junior. Menheniott was represented by Mr. T.G. Field-Fisher, Q.C., with Graham Neville in support.

Bodmin is a small market town some thirty miles or so from the Devon border and the granite court building is in the centre of the town. The square, austere courthouse must be a forbidding place for the less optimistically-minded defendant. There are two identical court rooms and Menheniott was to spend long hours in the dock of Number 1 Court before he would know his fate. Each court had two common factors: terrible accoustics and grey painted walls.

At 10.30 a.m. everyone rose as the Judge entered court and took his seat, with the Jury Box to his left and the witness box to his right. As he looked down at the assembled lawyers before him he saw, standing behind them in the large wooden dock, the heavily-built Defendant flanked by two prison officers. The Jury of ten men and two women were then sworn in by the Clerk of the Court, who then put the charges to the black-bearded Menheniott. He pleaded Not Guilty to murder, Not Guilty to four charges of intentionally causing Stephen grievous bodily harm and Not Guilty to disposing of Stephen's body with the intention of preventing the Coroner from holding an Inquest, a plea which he changed during the course of the trial.

Mr. Owen-Thomas, opening for the Crown, referred to the charge of disposing of Stephen's body with the intention of preventing a coroner's inquest: "You may wonder why a man should do that if he had nothing to fear," he said. "Those who do nothing wrong have nothing to fear."

Counsel referred to Mrs. Elizabeth Rayner as a "woman very much under the influence of her father," and described Stephen as "rather slow, weakly and puny in contrast to his robust father."

During Counsel's opening speech to the jury, Mr. Owen-Thomas produced the dead youth's skull and four of his broken ribs to illustrate injuries Stephen had received from blows inflicted by his father. "We say," said prosecuting counsel, "that during the last six months of the lad's life he was subjected to acts of violence of a vicious and deliberate nature. There was one occasion when Stephen did not do something he was told to do and his father picked up a length of tubular scaffolding and hit the lad across the back with it. And after this incident and other incidents you will hear about, Stephen was unable to stand up properly and was not allowed to go out in case anybody should see the marks on him and begin to ask questions."

Mr. Owen-Thomas admitted that the Prosecution could not prove exactly when Stephen died. He was alive on Boxing Day, 1975, but at the beginning of March 1976 he was not there when his younger sister, Margaret, visited Holy Vale. "For what happened on the last day of the boy's life we have to rely on the evidence of his other sister, Mrs. Rayner. She will tell you how her father hit Stephen across the face one evening and how she later found her brother lying cold and moaning on the floor of his bedroom. She asked her father if they could get a doctor, but he said no. Then at three o'clock in the morning the accused found his son dead in his bedroom." Counsel invited the Jury to ask themselves why Menheniott had refused to call a doctor and why he refused to give the boy a proper funeral.

The only witness called on the first day of the trial was the dental surgeon, Barrie Fairest, who had been practicing on St. Mary's for seventeen years. He told Mr. Owen-Thomas that he had carried out routine dental work on Stephen's teeth in November and December, 1974. In August, 1975 Stephen attended at the surgery again, but as a complicated filling was necessary and there was insufficient time to carry it out a new appointment was made and Stephen accordingly returned to the surgery on 28th October, 1975. It was at this stage that Mr. Fairest began to get worried, because he immediately noticed that four of Stephen's upper front teeth had been damaged in varying degrees. Mr. Owen-Thomas handed Mr. Fairest the skull and he indicated the teeth in question. Mr. Fairest's view was that "three of the teeth were damaged to the extent that in my opinion they were not reasonably repairable." Between a half and two-thirds of those three teeth above the gum line had broken off. The fourth tooth was damaged to a lesser extent.

When asked by Counsel what degree of force or violence would be necessary to cause this damage, Mr. Fairest replied, "It is difficult to break a tooth. It is possible to break a tooth with a very small force applied with a small, very hard object. The typical example is someone drinking from a bottle and someone nudges their elbow, they tap the tooth and it will shatter, but here we have four teeth which had been damaged over an arc. It was not, I felt, conceivable that a small hard object had damaged those teeth. It would have required significant force, a blow from some fairly hard substance, to break those four teeth." Asked what sort of a blow he envisaged, the dentist replied that "it was entirely compatible with a fist blow to the face. I have seen this before." Mr. Fairest also recalled that Stephen's upper lip was swollen and lacerated, and again he felt that the cause of this was entirely compatible with a blow being received on the mouth. He had, in fact, questioned Stephen about the injuries but the Jury were not allowed to hear the details of that conversation owing to the hearsay rule of evidence. But Mr. Justice Willis wanted his opinion.

"My opinion was simply that he had received a blow or blows to the face."

Mr. Fairest said that he made another appointment for Stephen and the three substantially damaged teeth were extracted on 8th November, 1975, and on 15th November he repaired the fourth tooth. Ten days later Stephen returned to the surgery and it was clear that he had received a further blow to the face and his denture was broken and there were further abrasions to the lip. According to the witness, similar force was necessary to break a denture as a natural tooth. He mended the denture and Stephen collected it on 26th November, and that was the last occasion he saw him as a patient.

In answer to Mr. Owen-Thomas, Mr. Fairest agreed that in addition to being a dental surgeon he was also a part-time fireman.

"On 18th May, 1977 did you go in your capacity as part-time fireman to California Field, Holy Vale, St. Mary's?"

"I did."

"Is that a piece of land which is given to be rather swampy?"

"Very close to a stream, very swampy."

"And in your fireman capacity were you there, if necessary, to operate pumps to clear away extra water?"

"Yes."

"Had you also taken something else with you?"

"I had."

"What was that?" asked Mr. Owen-Thomas.

"In anticipation of the event, I had taken with me Stephen Menheniott's records and one or two necessary instruments with which to examine anything which might be found."

"And were you present when digging commenced and remains were found?"

"Yes."

"Digging commenced under the supervision of Dr. Hunt - is that right?" asked Mr. Owen-Thomas.

"Dr. Hunt was present, Sir, yes."

"While the body was still in the grave did you examine any part of it?"

"I examined the teeth."

"You had your records?"

"I had copies of my records, and my original records but I did not use those too closely," replied the dentist.

"Were you able, from the examination of the treatment that had been given to the deceased, positively to say that that was Stephen Menheniott?"

"There was no doubt in my opinion that that was Stephen Menheniott, although I was not able to do a thoroughly formal examination at that time. There was no point of disagreement and many points of agreement."

Stephen's skull was again handed to Mr. Fairest, who went on to explain that when he was examining the body in the grave he found that the front tooth which he had repaired, and also the right canine tooth, were missing and it was his opinion "that they had been dislodged from the skull with some violence close to the time of death." He said that he "would expect there to be evidence of healing had they been expelled further away from the time of death."

The dentist told the jury that one's top teeth fit into sockets of bone known as the labial plate and in respect of the missing right canine tooth the bony socket was totally missing which meant "that the tooth was dislodged from the head with considerable force." He agreed with Mr. Owen-Thomas that something like two-thirds or more of the total length of a canine tooth goes into the socket and he felt that these two teeth were more likely to have been knocked out with two blows rather than one, and that considerable force would have been needed, force which could have been generated by a fist. At this stage, Stephen's skull was passed to the Jury for examination, a duty which some of them at least found disconcerting.

Mr. Owen-Thomas asked Mr. Fairest in relation to the two missing teeth, "If the teeth had been expelled after death while the body was lying in the grave, what would you expect to find?"

"No doubt had they been expelled after death whilst in the grave, I would expect to have found those teeth in the mouth, or what remained of the mouth."

"I take it you did not?"

"I did not, Sir."

"Was the grave in the area of the head searched carefully?"

"The whole area of the head was examined carefully because we were looking for those teeth. We did not find them."

Mr. Fairest then indicated that the next day, 19th May, 1977, he had been present when Dr. Hunt, the Home Office Pathologist, carried out a post-mortem examination on the remains. The witness said that he had examined the available teeth, and he confirmed that "the fillings which I had inserted were plain and easy to see and to identify as my work," and he added that he "had no doubt that this was Stephen Menheniott."

DAY TWO

Soon after this opinion had been delivered, the Court adjourned and resumed the following day with Mr. Field-Fisher commencing his cross-

44

cross-examination of Mr. Fairest. The witness agreed that he had never been concerned about the boy's general health as opposed to his dental health. "Had I felt that he was suffering from malnutrition to the point that it endangered his health I would have done something about it. I was aware that he was a thin boy and I was not happy about his condition, but it was not severe enough to ask for further attention."

Mr. Field-Fisher: "It is a small island and a small community and, of course, you know the doctors perfectly well?"

"Yes."

"And indeed on none of those occasions, except in direct relation to the injuries that you have explained to us about the teeth and the mouth, did you see any other sort of injury or bruise on him?"

"It is not easy to see, to observe or to be aware of, bruising on a fully-clothed, fully-dressed person. I was not aware of any injuries on any of the areas of the body which were visible to me."

Questions were then put to Mr. Fairest concerning his opinion that the injuries to the teeth were consistent with having been caused by a blow or blows with a fist. Mr. Fairest confirmed his view and added, "I have seen, possibly in my student days rather than recently, half-a-dozen to a dozen cases of such injuries. The best description I can give of these injuries is to say that they were entirely compatible with other occasions when it has been an acknowledged blow or blows to the face with a fist."

It was clear that Counsel was not going to get any assistance with that line of questioning and he sensibly changed tack: "When the body was revealed in the grave, was it lying on its back or partly sideways?"

"On its back."

"And the head - was that turned to the side?"

"No, Sir."

"There was nothing to protect the body: it was not enclosed in anything?"

"Clothing, but not on the head area."

"That is what I mean. There would be nothing to protect the face or the teeth when the hole was filled in?"

"I do not know, Sir. There could have been tissue there which disintegrated. There was none visible when the body was removed."

Mr. Fairest agreed that the grave was about two feet deep and it was put to him that anyone who was concerned to see that the grave should not show too much above the surface would be anxious to stamp down the material that had been thrown back on the grave.

"I would accept that."

"If that were done and done with some force, that might well have the effect of breaking any of the teeth in the skull immediately underneath, might it not?"

"In my opinion impossible, Sir."

"Not possible?" queried Mr. Field-Fisher.

"Not possible."

"Why do you say that?"

"I say that because the thickness of material between the face and the surface would be sufficient to cushion the blow. The material itself was of a soft, almost pliable clay, which perhaps one could describe as being a very effective shock insulator; almost as effective as some of the packings which I use for delicate appliances."

"It depends whether there were stones there?"

"I was not aware of any stones there. It was a marshy area and the material was very largely of this white clay. I remember I did some of the digging and clearing myself and was watching intently the whole time. I cannot swear there were no stones there, Sir, but I am jolly nearly certain that there were none and it was simply clay."

"If there was evidence that after the grave was filled in, a tractor went over the grave would that make a difference to your opinion?"

"The spreading of a load on a tractor tyre is considerable. It is a wide tyre at the rear. The front does not carry an enormous amount of the weight. The soil itself is soft, the clay is soft and mushy. I am equally sure this would not have broken those teeth."

Mr. Justice Willis, addressing himself to Mr. Field-Fisher interposed: "I think one must be very specific. I find it very difficult, probably the Jury do, to know exactly what you are putting. Are you putting a tractor wheel..."

Mr. Field-Fisher, "Yes."

"... going straight over the face?"

Mr. Field-Fisher, "Yes, I am."

"May I make a two point observation?" enquired Mr. Fairest. "First of all, to answer your question, I think it is less likely that a tractor wheel would inflict this damage to those teeth than the tamping we have discussed before, and secondly, I had occasion to view that spot several months prior (to the body being recovered) and that area had not changed. It is a fairly constant soggy area of the field."

"Of course," remarked Counsel, "a few months before what you are talking about would have put the date back to some time in February or March or April. No doubt there would be a bit of rain then?"

"It is an area within ten feet of a nature walk," Mr. Fairest replied. "It is an enjoyable walk. I have taken that walk frequently with my family and I specifically looked at that area a few months before and then it looked no different from the way it looked at this time, an area of sogginess. That area goes down to an open pond which has an open drain to the sea and I have known this area very well now for twenty years. We picnic, we enjoy ourselves there. The water level does not significantly vary in that small valley."

"Well now, if the tractor was used to go across and around that grave for the purpose of dragging a log there to cover the grave up, your view is that that would not materially alter your opinion that that could not cause damage to the face underneath?"

"From my knowledge of that area, and from my viewing of the body, I am ever more certain that a tractor could not cause that damage."

Here, Mr. Field-Fisher, referring to a photograph and to a plan of the area prepared by the police, pointed out a tree by the flower packing shed just down a track from the cottage. He said there were signs of branches having been lopped, and put to Mr. Fairest that "it would be perfectly possible, would it not, to cause the kind of injury to one's mouth that Stephen in fact had if he fell out of the tree?"

Mr. Fairest replied that "it would be very possible to cause that kind of injury but very difficult to do that and no other physical injury."

Mr. Field-Fisher then postulated the theory that the damage to Stephen's teeth might have been caused by him hitting a branch of the tree during the process of falling out of the tree. Mr. Fairest said that the damage to the teeth did not seem compatible with that type of injury, but agreed that it was a possibility and that he could not exclude it. Mr. Fairest, indeed, went on to say that this was one of the possible causes of the injury which he considered on two occasions when he saw Stephen: "On both occasions I did not accept, after some consideration, that this was even vaguely likely to be the cause of his injuries."

At this stage, Mr. Field-Fisher indicated to the Judge that he would like to raise a matter in the absence of the Jury. The point of the submission was obviously going to relate to Mr. Fairest's comment that he had considered, when treating Stephen, whether the dental injuries could have been caused in a tree climbing accident. Why, the Jury might be asking themselves, should he have considered such a possibility unless Stephen had told him that his injuries had indeed been caused in that manner? The obstacle to the success of such a submission was the 'hearsay rule' referred to earlier.

When the Jury had withdrawn, Mr. Field-Fisher made this very point and said that in his evidence before the Isles of Scilly Justices, Mr. Fairest had said that on two occasions Stephen had told him that his injuries had been caused in that very manner, and that it was just because of this that the dental surgeon had considered and then rejected that as a real probability. Menheniott's Counsel clearly wished the Jury to be told of Stephen's comments at the surgery because that might, in the Jury's eyes, tend to show that all Stephen's injuries had not been caused by his father. Counsel conceded that the rules of evidence did not normally allow such evidence to be given, but told the Judge that this was a very unusual case.

Mr. Field-Fisher said that if indeed Stephen had told Mr. Fairest in the surgery that the injuries had been caused by him falling out of a tree, there might be a number of reasons why he said it. "He may have said it because he was in great fear of his father and was told that he had to say it. It may, on the other hand, be that it was perfectly genuinely said, which is, of course, the way the Defence put it. That is a matter the Jury have got to make up their mind about."

"Now, I would wish to ask Mr. Fairest what he was actually told by Stephen as to how he got his injuries. I suggest it is relevant in this case and admissible because he has based his appraisal of the situation not upon a hypothesis that came to him out of the blue but upon something that he was actually told by his patient."

Mr. Justice Willis: "There is another way of looking at it. Supposing Stephen told him that the injuries had been caused by blows received from his father?"

Mr. Field-Fisher replied, "That would not be admissible against the father. That is perfectly plain."

After further legal argument, Mr. Justice Willis asked Mr. Owen-Thomas what he had to say. Counsel said that in his submission, evidence of what Stephen had said as to the cause of his injuries was not admissible. The Jury were entitled to have the best evidence before them. Mr. Field-Fisher's submission was an attempt to get in evidence which was secondary evidence and inadmissible and it depended upon the truthfulness of the boy at the time. Furthermore, it would be improper to admit hearsay evidence simply because it assisted the Defence. Mr. Owen-Thomas concluded by saying, "I do not wish to be obstructive here, but if it is sought to prove that this boy fell from a tree and sustained these injuries and someone saw him do it, then that evidence should be called and I object to this method of trying to get in that in a secondary manner."

Mr. Justice Willis asked Mr. Field-Fisher, "You do not wish to add anything?"

"No, my Lord," he replied. "Hearsay is of course not admissible - one knows that - even to assist the Defence. When one talks about the best evidence it is difficult to think of better evidence as to the cause of an injury than that spoken by somebody himself. My Learned Friend says we do not know whether he said it. This witness has said on oath already at the committal hearing that he did in fact say it on two occasions. My Lord, on that basis, although technically it is secondary evidence, I submit it is difficult to see what better evidence there could be."

Mr. Justice Willis: "No, I am against you, Mr. Field-Fisher." The Judge's ruling was clearly correct in law, but it was certainly a major setback for the defence team.

The Jury returned to Court and after Mr. Field-Fisher had asked Mr. Fairest a few more questions, Mr. Owen-Thomas rose to re-examine him. He asked him why he had earlier said that he was not worried about Stephen's general health but was not happy about his condition.

Mr. Fairest replied that "a dentist's job largely consists of coping with fear. One becomes very used to observing, evaluating and handling patients who are nervous. This patient's demeanour in many ways on most of the occasions on which I saw him caused me to be seriously concerned for his welfare, sufficiently seriously concerned for his welfare for me to take certain actions and certain, if I may use the word, preparations because of the depth of my concern for the boy. He was frightened."

"If the deceased was lying in the grave on his back," asked Mr. Owen-Thomas, "with his head up and the lower jaw in position, and pressure was applied to the face, if that pressure was of sufficient force to cause these teeth to be dislodged so that the labial plate was broken in the way this was, would you or would you not expect any other bony injury to the face?"

"There are two answers. Yes, you are right, I would expect there to be other injuries but, again, emphatically I do not consider that the tractor could in any way have caused that. I am quite adamant about that."

"Yes," Mr. Owen-Thomas persisted, "but assuming for the moment you are wrong, what other sort of injury would one expect to find if that degree of force had been applied when this body was lying in the grave? If that degree of force had been applied, what other bony injury might one find to the face?"

"I would have expected other teeth to be affected. I would expect the bone of the maxilla to be damaged in some way - the maxilla being the upper jaw bone, that which supports those teeth." Such additional injuries were not present.

After a few closing questions from prosecuting counsel in relation to the state of the ground in California Field, Mr. Fairest left the witness box. His evidence had been clearly given and there was no doubt that he had impressed the Court with his professionalism.

The tension noticeably increased as the next witness entered court: Elizabeth Anne Rayner, (Liz), Menheniott's daughter, who was known to have been closely involved in Stephen's last hours. Because of the effect of her recent stroke she had to be taken through her evidence very slowly.

In answer to prosecuting counsel's questions she confirmed that she was born on 14th July, 1952, that she had spent much of her life in Homes or in Care, that she had finally returned to Holy Vale in 1970 and that Stephen finally returned there in 1972.

She said that her father's violence to Stephen started as soon as he returned to the Island in 1972.

"How," asked Mr. Owen-Thomas, "did your father treat Stephen?"

"He was always rough with him."

"In what sort of ways? No, do not bother to look at him (her father), you look towards the Jury. In what sort of way was he rough with him?"

"Violence."

"Violence? How did the violence show itself?"

"Temper."

"And what happened when there was the violence? What happened to Stephen?"

"He used to get sick."

"Did that happen often or not?"

"Yes, it did."

"What did your father hit Stephen with?" asked Mr. Owen-Thomas.

"Anything he could lay his hands on."

"Did he ever hit him with his hands?"

"Yes."

"And what sort of form did his hand take at that time? Was it open or closed, or what?"

"Open."

"Did you ever see it when clenched?"

"No."

"And when he hit him and used the violence, did it seem to you when you saw it to be hard or not?"

"Yes."

"And what often used to happen to Stephen after he had been hit hard by your father? Where would Stephen end up?"

"On the floor."

"Was this something that happened rarely or something that happened often?"

"Often."

"Have you ever seen any marks on Stephen?"

"Yes, I did."

"Where on him have you seen marks?"

"On his back."

Counsel asked Mrs. Rayner to tell the court about some of the implements which her father had used against Stephen. She said he had used a metal scaffolding pipe, a shovel and a broom handle. So far as the scaffolding pipe incident was concerned, this happened on the farm about a week before Stephen was buried. Stephen would not do what he was told and his father picked up the piping which just happened to be lying in a field by the greenhouses and "took a swipe at him."

"And where did it hit him?"

"Across his back."

"And what happened to Stephen?"

"He collapsed," she replied, "and stayed on the ground for about five minutes."

"After that incident was he allowed to go out, out from the house?"

"No."

"Who prevented him going out from the house?"

"My father."

"Did he say why Stephen was not to go out?"

"He was afraid that people might talk."

"People might talk about what?"

"He had an injury to his mouth."

In connection with the shovel incident, Mrs. Rayner said that this happened about a week before the scaffolding assault and occurred when father and son were out flower picking near California Field.

"And what caused your father to hit Stephen with the shovel?" Counsel asked.

"He would not pick the flowers fast enough."

"And, having picked up the shovel, what did he do?"

"He swiped at him."

"And did it hit him?"

"Yes, it did."

"Where?"

"Across his back again."

"And what happened to Stephen?"

"He doubled up with it."

"Did he stay on his feet?"

"No."

"And how long did he stay down?"

"About five minutes."

"Did he get up?"

"He did with my help."

At this point, Counsel was handed a broken broomstick by a court usher, and in answer to Mr. Owen-Thomas's questions, Mrs. Rayner said it had been kept at Holy Vale and had been broken when her father hit Stephen with it in the passageway of the house about two days before he died. As a result of the blow, Stephen fell against the wall. Mrs. Rayner also confirmed that Stephen's teeth were damaged - "My Dad used to hit him across the face with the palm of his hand."

Mrs. Rayner went on to tell the court that on the evening of Stephen's death, father and son had a row in the passage of the house and her father hit Stephen across his back and face a number of times, causing him to fall to the floor.

"When Stephen had been knocked to the ground," Counsel asked, "did he stay on the ground for some time or not?"

"Yes, he did."

"And about how long was he lying there?"

"I do not know; about five minutes."

"And what happened to your father?"

51

"He went upstairs to bed."

"What happened to Stephen? How did he get up?"

"I helped him up."

"And when you helped him up, where did he go?"

"He went into the bathroom to have a bath."

"Did he have a bath?" Counsel enquired.

"Yes, he did," replied Mrs. Rayner.

"Did you see him in the bath?"

"Yes."

"That night?" asked Counsel.

"Yes."

"Did you see any marks on him?"

"Yes, I did."

"Where?"

"On his back."

"Had he got some sort of complaint with his legs at the time?"

"Yes."

"Something wrong with his legs, and was he having some sort of treatment for that from your father?"

"Yes, he was."

"Did he go that evening to have something done to his legs?"

"Yes."

"Was that before he had his bath or afterwards?"

"Afterwards."

"And how was he dressed?"

"Maybe in pyjamas, I am not sure."

"Did he go somewhere to have his legs attended to?"

"My father's bedroom."

"How did he put his leg forward for treatment? What happened?" asked Mr. Owen-Thomas.

"Hold on to the door and put his leg forward," she replied, looking towards the dock.

The Judge, the Defence and the Jury were clearly finding Mrs. Rayner's replies difficult to hear and she had been frequently warned to keep her voice up and not to look at her father.

"Listen to me," said Mr. Owen-Thomas, "and do not worry about Mr. Menheniott. Now you just listen to me. On this occasion he came into the bedroom. Then you say, he held on to the door and put one of his legs forward - is that right?"

"That is correct."

"And where was your father?"

"On the bed."

"And what did he do so far as Stephen's leg was concerned?"

"Put powder on it and put cotton wool on it."

52

"Did he put a bandage round it?"

"Yes, he did."

"That was one leg. What about the second leg?"

"The same thing."

"He was holding on to the door, you said, with one leg forward so that he was balancing on the other leg - is that right?"

"Yes."

"Now," said Counsel, "I want you to think very carefully about this. Did he remain on one or other leg the whole time?"

Counsel was clearly anticipating Mrs. Rayner to confirm that her father had pulled Stephen's leg away from him, because in evidence before the Isles of Scilly Justices she had said: "Stephen wouldn't stand still and father pulled him and he fell backwards and hit his head on the wall." Now, however, in reply to counsel's question, she merely replied, "Yes."

She said that after he had had his legs bandaged, Stephen returned to his bedroom whilst she remained in her father's bedroom watching the television.

"And while you were watching the television did you hear something?"

"Yes. Stephen was moaning."

"You heard Stephen moaning. Did you go from your father's bedroom when you heard Stephen moaning?"

"Yes."

"Where did you go?"

"Stephen's room."

"And where was he?"

"In his own room."

"And how long was this after he had had his legs done?"

"About ten minutes."

"And when you went to his bedroom and you found him there, where was he in the bedroom?"

"Lying on a cold floor."

"What did you do?"

"Told him to get on his bed."

"Did he?"

"No."

Mrs. Rayner told the court that her father had also heard the moaning at the same time as she had and he told her to go in and stop him as there were visitors in the next door cottage.

"When you could not get him to go on his bed, did you try to lift him up at all?"

"No."

"Did you go back to your father's bedroom?"

"Yes."

"Did you tell him?"

"Yes, I did."

"What did you tell him?"

"That he was lying on a cold floor naked."

"Nothing on at all?"

"No."

"What did your father say?"

"Did not say anything."

"Well, did the moaning go on or not?"

"Yes, it did."

"Did you go back to see Stephen at all?"

"Yes."

"Why?"

"Because of the blow he had that evening."

"Which blow was that?"

"The one round his face."

"What was it that worried you about the blow round his face that made you go back again and see him in the bedroom?"

"Because his mouth was bleeding."

"Did you see that the first time that you went in there to him?"

"Yes."

"Did you see it when he came in to have his legs treated?"

"Yes."

"When you went back in again, you say because he was continuing to moan, was he in the same place?"

"Yes, he was."

"Were you worried about him or not?"

"Yes."

"Did you know there were two doctors on St. Mary's."

"Yes."

"Did you or did you not think about a doctor?"

"Yes, I did think about a doctor."

"Did you go back to your father's bedroom?"

"Yes, I did."

"Did you tell him that he was still lying on the floor?"

"Yes."

"Did you say anything about the blood coming from his mouth?"

"No."

"Why not?"

"Because my father was not interested."

"Did you say anything about a doctor?"

"Yes, I did. I asked him to get one down to see him."

"And what did your father say?"

"No."

"How far did the nearer of the two doctors live from your house?"

"About five minutes."

"Did you continue then for the time being to be in your father's bedroom?"

"Yes."

"Did the moaning go on or not?"

"All night."

"Did you go back at all again? How many times did you go in to him that night?"

"Nearly every hour."

"And was he moaning the whole time?"

"Yes, he was."

Mrs. Rayner said that her father also went to see Stephen and that after she had been in to see him two or three times they managed to lift him on to his bed and she put some blankets round him.

"Next morning was Stephen still alive?"

"No."

"When did you know that Stephen was dead?"

"My father came round at three o'clock in the early morning and told me he was dead?"

"Did he say anything then, or about that time, to you about a funeral?"

"He said, 'Sorry, Liz, we can't have a funeral or have a doctor.' "

"Did you say 'Why'?"

"No."

"Why did you not ask 'Why can't he have a funeral or doctor?' "

"The reason why he could not have a doctor was because of the marks on his back."

"Well, did your father say what was going to happen to Stephen or Stephen's body?"

"He said he had two choices. One was to bury him down the farm. The other was to put him over Deep Point, into the sea."

Mrs. Rayner told the court that she tied Stephen's bedroom door up after she knew he was dead to stop her eldest boy from going in there. She also said that the day after he died her father told her that he had decided to bury Stephen and that if anyone asked after him she was to say he had gone to the mainland to see his girlfriend in Sussex. Her father started to dig a grave in a field but the ground was too hard and he then decided to dig the grave down in the marshes in California Field.

"Did your father dig a grave in California Field?"

"Yes."

"Stephen meantime had still been in his bedroom, had he?"

"Yes."

"Lying there dead."

Stephen Menheniott picking daffodils on his father's farm on St. Mary's

Mr. Barrie Fairest the St. Mary's dental surgeon who treated Stephen's teeth and examined the body in the grave.

"Yes."

"Did you help in carrying him out of the house?"

"Yes, I did."

"And where was he put first of all?"

"Into the boot of a car."

"And to where was he taken in the car?"

"To the greenhouse field on the farm."

"Was the body taken out of the boot?"

"Yes."

"Where was it put?"

"On to a tarpaulin."

"On to a tarpaulin, and then...?"

"On to a wheelbarrow."

"And then was it taken to the grave?"

"Yes, it was."

"Was it put into the grave."

"Yes."

"You were there, were you?"

"Yes."

"And the earth was put over the top of it?"

"Yes."

Mr. Justice Willis: "Mr. Owen-Thomas, did you ask the witness what time of day this was?"

"No, my Lord, I did not."

Mr. Owen-Thomas then asked Mrs. Rayner: "When was it, in the day or evening or night, that this was done?"

"Midnight."

"Did your father tell you why it was being done then?"

"So nobody would see us."

"Did something happen with a log after the earth had been shovelled over Stephen?"

"A log was put over the top of it to stop people seeing it from the nature trail."

"Does it go along quite close to the place where this grave was dug?"

"Yes, it does."

"And later on, in fact, did you plant some bulbs on top of the grave?"

"Yes."

"Now, at the time that he died your brother was in receipt of money from the Social Security people, was he not?"

"Yes."

"And did your father say what he would do so far as the Social Security were concerned?"

58

"Write to them."

"Do you remember the time when you and your father realised you would have to leave Holy Vale?"

"Yes."

"That was because Mr. Gibson had died?"

Mr. Gibson, it will be recalled, was Menheniott's landlord.

"Yes."

"Was that in December, 1976?"

"Yes."

"And", Mr. Owen-Thomas continued, "at that time, when you knew you would have to go, did your father say something to you about the grave and Stephen's body?"

"He was going to move it."

"Did he say why he was going to move it?"

"Because whoever took over the farm would find the body."

Counsel then said he wished to go back to the question of Stephen's damaged teeth. Did her father tell her what to say if anyone asked how the damage occured? "Yes," she replied, "That it happened when he fell out of a tree." She also said that it was she who persuaded Stephen to go and see the dentist. Her father had not wanted him to go as he was afraid of trouble, of people talking.

"Did you," enquired Mr. Owen-Thomas, "sometimes tidy up Stephen's bedroom?"

"Yes."

"Did you ever see anything on the pillowcase?"

"Blood."

"And how often did you see blood on Stephen's pillowcase?"

"Nearly every day."

"Apart from the bleeding of the mouth that you told us about on that last evening, did you ever see blood or anything else coming from Stephen's head or any part of his head?"

"From his ears."

"What was it you saw coming from his ears?"

"Yellow stuff. Every day."

Counsel went on to elicit from Mrs. Rayner that Menheniott used to hit Stephen about the ears, and this caused the ears in some way to burst and the 'yellow stuff' to come out.

Counsel then had a final try at getting further facts from the witness in respect of the leg-treating session on the last night of Stephen's life, about which Mrs. Rayner had not previously been particularly forthcoming.

"How did Stephen leave your father's bedroom that time?"

"He crawled."

"Well, how had he come in? You had gone to fetch him. Had he walked in or crawled in?"

"Walked in."

"What had happened that made him crawl out?"

"Stephen was standing up holding onto the door and he would not keep still and Dad pulled his leg and he fell back and hit his head on the wall."

"From what you could see, did it seem necessary to pull his leg in that way just to put the powder and bandages on the leg?"

"No."

"After he had been hit on the occasion with the scaffold pipe, you said that after a bit he got up. Was he able to lift things easily after that?"

"No."

"Well, what sort of things would he have to lift up?"

"A can of diesel for the tractor."

"And had he," enquired Counsel, "been able to do that fairly easily before he had been hit with the scaffold pipe?"

"Yes."

"After he had been hit with the scaffold pipe he was not able to do that so easily - is that what you are saying?"

"Yes."

"Were there other things that he was not able to lift?"

"Yes, there were. Bags of bulbs."

"What about walking - any difference in his walking after he had been hit with the scaffold pipe?"

"He used to lean over like a humpback."

"Did he do that before?"

"No."

After one or two further routine questions to tidy up her evidence, Mr. Owen-Thomas concluded Mrs. Rayner's evidence-in-chief.

DAY THREE

Elizabeth now had to prepare herself for cross-examination the following day by Mr. Field-Fisher. It can safely be assumed that she was finding the whole business of attending court a traumatic experience. Most witnesses tend to worry and be nervous, but here was a witness who was not only giving evidence against her father, with whom she had had a close relationship, but who even at her young age, and she was only 25 years old at the time of the trial, had already suffered a stroke and who was still very far from well. It will be recalled, for instance, that only four months earlier she had entered the courthouse on St. Mary's with the help of a three-legged walking aid when giving evidence at the preliminary hearing. Mr. Field-Fisher, as well as being an advocate, is a part-time Judge of the Crown Court and often sits in his judicial capacity at the Bodmin Crown Court. He is a kindly and understanding man who would undoubtedly, within the terms of his brief, treat her as sympathetically as possible.

He began his cross-examination by endeavouring to reconcile conflicting evidence as to the dates of the scaffolding and shovel incidents. It was important for him to try and establish that if assaults took place, that they took place as long before death as possible, since that would help him to persuade the Jury that they played no part in the cause of death and should thus be ignored.

So far as the scaffolding assault was concerned, Mrs. Rayner had told the Justices at the committal hearing that it took place "about two months before Stephen died," but in the Crown Court she had, of course, said it took place "about a week" before his death. She now agreed that what she had said at the committal hearing was correct.

Concerning the incident with the shovel, she had told prosecuting counsel in the Crown Court that it occurred about two weeks before the death. In her evidence before the magistrates she had said, "This incident with the shovel was at about the same time as the incident with the scaffolding," namely about two months before his death. She now told defence counsel that she stood by what she had said on St. Mary's.

Mr. Field-Fisher had started well, but one had the clear impression, possibly because of the effects of her stroke, that Mrs. Rayner had a tendency to agree with anything that was put to her.

Counsel went on to ask her whether Stephen was sometimes a very irritating boy.

"Yes."

"And your father has a rather quick temper, does he not?"

"Yes."

"It is a temper that blows up quickly and subsides quickly?"

"Yes."

"Now, on those two occasions that you have spoken of, Stephen, you say, fell to the ground but he was able to get up; I think you said you helped him on one occasion - is that right?"

"Yes."

"Did he go on working?"

"Yes."

Counsel then proceeded to deal with the marks that Mrs. Rayner had seen on Stephen's back. He got an admission from her that she had only seen one mark on his back and that it was the size of a 50p. piece and brown in colour. This was about a month before he died when she had seen him naked in the bath. She disagreed, however, with Counsel's suggestion that the mark had always been on Stephen's back. She had seen his back sometimes when his shirt pulled up and the mark had not been there.

"Now I want to ask you about the broomstick," Mr. Field-Fisher said. "I suggest that there was some sort of an incident involving your father and Stephen, the broomstick was picked up by your father, he took a shot at Stephen but he broke the broomstick on the bannisters. Now, is that what happened?"

"No," replied Mrs. Rayner.

"I suggest to you that you are wrong about the shovel incident, that you never saw your father deliberately strike Stephen with it. What do you say about that suggestion?"

"It did happen."

"Did it happen exactly as you say it happened or is the fact, for instance, that your father may have thrown the shovel?"

"No."

"And so far as the scaffold pole is concerned, again I suggest that you are wrong about that: he did not actually hit him with it at all. What do you say about that?"

"He did."

At this point Mr. Field-Fisher obtained confirmation from Mrs. Rayner that it was she who stopped Stephen from going out, so that people would not ask questions, with her father merely agreeing to her suggestion, and that this proposal only came about in relation to the damage to Stephen's mouth and not in connection with any of the other incidents.

"Now it is right, is it not," counsel continued, "that you never saw your father use his fist on Stephen's face; he used his open hand?"

"That is correct."

"Did you actually see any teeth knocked out?"

"No."

"You were not present when whatever happened to Stephen caused his teeth to come out?"

"No."

"Is it right that at that time there was lopping of trees going on?"

"Yes there was."

"That would be some time in the late summer or autumn of the year before he died?"

"Yes."

"And one tree in particular that was being lopped, I expect you will remember, is the one where there was a block and tackle on it, over by the buildings where the packing shed is. Do you remember that?"

"Yes, I do."

"You remember the tree in particular. Was that a tree that was being lopped at that time?"

"No."

"Well, which tree do you say was being lopped at that time?"

"One behind the greenhouse."

"What was the block and tackle doing on that tree then?"

"Father used to strip down engines of cars."

"And he would use the block and tackle for that?"

"Yes."

Counsel then put to Mrs. Rayner that it appeared from the police photograph of the tree which had the block and tackle attached to it, and which had been taken at the time of the discovery of the body, that it had recently been lopped. She did not, however, agree.

"Now," said Counsel, "all I am asking you is this: if that tree was not kept properly lopped from time to time, it would make it more difficult for lorries to get round the corner to the packing shed. Now, is that not right?"

"Yes."

"And when you became aware of the damage to Stephen's mouth and broken teeth, your father told you that he had done it falling out of a tree."

"Yes."

"It is right, is it not, that that damage to his mouth was the only damage you saw to his mouth between then, (when Menheniott had mentioned to his daughter that Stephen had fallen out of a tree), which was the first time you saw it, and the time he died? You did not see any further damage to his mouth?"

"No."

Counsel now came to the crucial night of Stephen's death.

"You had all had your meal together. Stephen used to work about the house, did he not?"

"Yes."

"In addition to doing work in the fields?"

"Yes."

"What sort of things did he do in the house?"

"Used to do the dishes."

"Take the dog for a walk?"

"Yes."

"Help to look after your children?"

"Yes."

"Did he cook sometimes?"

"Yes."

"Was he," enquired Mr. Field-Fisher, "doing all these things perfectly normally up to the day he died, up till the night he died?"

"No, he was suffering."

"Suffering in what way - with his mouth, you mean, or his legs?"

"His legs."

"That was this sort of rash that he had?"

"Yes."

"Had he suffered from that in previous years?"

"No."

"It was a rash that some people do suffer from when they handle plants?"

"Yes."

"It is not unknown in the Islands, is it?"

"No."

"It is a nasty irritation?"

"Yes, it is."

"Very unpleasant?"

"Yes."

Mr. Justice Willis intervened to enquire its name and was told it was known as a flower rash.

"Flower rash," said Mr. Field-Fisher. "But apart from that he was in perfectly ordinary health."

"Yes."

"And that was true right up until the last night?"

"Yes."

"Had your father," asked Counsel, "been treating Stephen's legs for some time?"

"A couple of weeks," replied Mrs. Rayner.

"Why did your father do it? Why could not Stephen do it himself?"

"I don't know."

"He could have done it himself?"

"Yes, I suppose he could."

"I suppose your father was being kind to him, was he?"

"Yes."

"Well now," Counsel continued, "there was this row in the passage you say, and you have told us that Stephen got hit across his back with your father's hand. How was he hit?"

"Rabbit punches."

"You mean with the side of his hand?"

"Yes."

"What part of his back?"

"Middle."

"And you say he got hit across the face before that when he was standing up?"

"Yes."

"You helped him up and Stephen was all right?"

"Yes."

"He was able to go and take a bath by himself?"

"Yes."

"He was (then) able to go upstairs, go into his own bedroom and then you went and fetched him to have his legs done?"

"Yes."

"When he came into the bedroom to have his legs treated, did he seem perfectly normal except for his legs?"

"Yes."

Mr. Field-Fisher now came on to the moment when Stephen fell in his father's bedroom when his legs were being treated.

"When he hit his head on the wall, what sort of a bang was it - quite a bad one?"

"Yes."

"Could you see what part of his head was hit?"

"The back of it."

"Is it a solid wall?"

"Yes."

"And when he banged his head in that way, did he fall down?"

"Yes."

Mrs. Rayner, who had been allowed to sit in the witness box, confirmed her earlier evidence relating to seeing Stephen later that evening at hourly intervals, and that he was moaning & mumbling and was difficult to understand. She said she thought Stephen was in that condition because of the bang to his head. Mr. Field-Fisher was now coming to the end of his cross-examination but wished to clarify two points.

"You were asked (by Mr. Owen-Thomas) when you described how he had his leg pulled by your father and he lost his balance and hit his head, if it was really necessary for your father to have pulled his leg like that. Your father was not in a temper at that time, was he?"

"No, he had calmed down."

"He had calmed right down by that time. It was an accident, was it not?"

"Yes."

"You wanted to have a doctor and your father said 'no'. If your father had realised or thought that Stephen was very ill he would have called a doctor, would he not?" enquired Mr. Field-Fisher.

Mr. Justice Willis: "Is that a question she can answer?"

Mr. Field-Fisher, continuing, "knowing your father as you do?"

"No, he would not."

"He would not have called a doctor. Is that because he does not like doctors?"

"Yes."

"Does not believe in doctors himself?"

"Not really."

At this point, Mr. Field-Fisher sat down and Mr. Owen-Thomas rose to re-examine Menheniott's daughter.

"I want to ask you some questions, Mrs. Rayner. On the occasion that he was hit with the scaffold pole, was he doing something wrong or was he not doing something he should be doing?"

"Was not doing things right."

"What was it that he was not doing right?"

"Picking flowers."

"What was the matter with the way that he was picking flowers?"

"Picked them too short."

"And how far away were you from where he was picking the flowers?"

"Same field."

"From where you were, could you see what happened?"

"Yes."

"What did happen?"

Mrs. Rayner replied that "my father and Stephen were rowing over the flowers. He just picked up the scaffolding and swung it at him and Stephen fell to the ground."

"Did it hit him?"

"He hit him with it."

She confirmed that a similar scenario covered the shovel incident.

"Stephen was not a very strong boy," said Mr. Owen-Thomas, "and sometimes had difficulty in lifting things. After he had been hit with the scaffolding and then on another occasion with the shovel, did he lift things as well as he could before, or not as well?"

"Not as well," she replied.

Mrs. Rayner's ordeal in the witness box was now over and she was allowed to leave the court and return to her home in Redruth. Ill, frail and unsteady on her feet though she was, she had given her evidence well, notwithstanding the effects of the stroke suffered earlier in the year. But as she left the witness-box, she was a sad figure with unhappy memories.

The next prosecution witness to be called was Menheniott's eldest child, William George Menheniott, aged twenty-seven, who lived in Truro. He confirmed that since 1973 he had been visiting Holy Vale Cottage each year and that the last time he had seen Stephen was at Christmas, 1975.

"Generally," asked Mr. Elfer, who had taken over temporarily from Mr. Owen-Thomas, "how would you describe the way your father and Stephen got on?"

"Well, he used to treat Stephen like an au pair boy or a lackey. He did the housework and looked after Liz's children."

"And did you ever see your father do anything towards Stephen?"

"I have seen him hit many a time."

"And hit him how?"

"With his fist, hand. He used to throw things at him."

"And where would the fists or hands land on Stephen?"

"In the face, in the stomach, on the arm."

"Have you ever seen, during 1973 until Christmas 1975, your father use anything other than his fist on Stephen?"

66

"I saw him use a broomstick once." He also recounted how he had seen his father throw spoons, or anything he could lay his hands on, including a bread knife, at Stephen.

Counsel now took the witness on to Christmas, 1975. He and his wife had travelled to St. Mary's and were staying with his father-in-law. On the Boxing Day he and his wife had gone to spend the day at Holy Vale. On arrival, William noticed that Stephen had lost one tooth and that another one had been cut or half broken. He asked his father how this had come about and he replied that Stephen had fallen off his bike.

Another incident that William remembered was at tea-time the same day. Stephen was in the sitting room with his father and William, who was in the hallway, heard a slap. His father then left the sitting room and a little while later Stephen came out, but owing to the poorness of the light in the hall William noticed nothing unusual about him.

Under cross-examination by Mr. Field-Fisher, William got terribly confused about dates. He eventually agreed that in 1973 he had only seen Stephen for a few minutes and that nothing untoward had happened. In March and August, 1974, he stayed at Holy Vale and again he saw nothing unusual happening.

"So we have now got one incident or one occasion," remarked Counsel, "which is Boxing Day, 1975, and that is the first time that there had been any sort of incident involving violence between your father and Stephen since 1969 - when Stephen left the Island?"

"Yes."

"And on the Boxing Day of 1975 you heard a slap, is that right?"

"Yes, and I saw him throw a spoon at him."

"Was that at the table?"

"Yes."

"Did that hurt Stephen?"

"No, it missed him."

"And just to make it quite plain what we are talking about," commented Mr. Field-Fisher, "when you arrived at Holy Vale on Boxing Day, 1975 he already had damage to his front teeth?"

"Yes."

"And so far as all the other matters that you were telling us about and the other violence and so on, I suggest to you that is quite untrue, but in any event, it is all before 1969?"

"Yes."

"And of course you knew that Stephen went back into care at the end of 1969 and you would know as a matter of family history, although you were not there, that he came back in 1972?"

"Yes."

"And you know, I daresay, that when he came back in 1972 he was dead keen to come home, was he not?"

"Yes, because he had nowhere to go."

"And he wanted to come home to his father and his family?"

"Yes, he did not have nowhere to go."

"Yes, thank you."

In re-examination, Mr. Owen-Thomas said: "If you did not see him between 1969 and 1972, how did you know he was dead keen to go home?"

"I did not," William replied.

"Well that is what I rather wondered. Had he anywhere else to go?"

"At the time, no."

William Menheniott had not been a very impressive Crown witness, although to be fair, it is always difficult to recount facts which had occurred years earlier.

William's wife, Heather, was the next witness to be called by the prosecution and she also gave evidence relating to their visit to Holy Vale on Boxing Day, 1975.

"When you arrived there," asked Mr. Elfer, "did you see anything that you noticed about Stephen's face?"

"Yes."

"What was that?"

"He had a lot of bruises on his face."

"Where were the bruises?"

"Well, sort of over on his face."

"Your hand movement went over both cheeks and then across the front of your mouth. Could you explain to us where the bruises were?"

"Around his mouth. One of his front teeth was missing completely and one was half broken off."

"Was there," enquired Counsel, "anything more than simple bruising to the mouth?"

"Yes," replied Heather Menheniott, "bruising and a few cuts around the mouth above the lip."

"Were they bleeding?"

"No, but they looked as if they had been and had dried."

"What time did you leave that evening?"

"About ten o'clock."

"Had anything untoward happened between the Defendant and Stephen?"

"No."

"And I think it is right that you did not see Stephen again after that?"

"No."

Mr. Field-Fisher rose to cross-examine and asked, "Mrs. Menheniott, you had seen no violence of any sort between your father-in-law and Stephen?"

"Not in recent years, no."

68

"Since Stephen went away from home at the end of 1969?"

"Not since then. I saw violence when he was there before."

"Yes, but I am talking about since 1969. We know from the dates that he came back in 1968 and was there for about thirteen months and then went away again towards the end of 1969, and you have not seen any violence of any sort between your father-in-law and him since then, have you?"

"Only shouting."

"Yes, but I am talking about violence."

"No."

This concluded Mrs. Menheniott's evidence and she left the witness box to be followed by Mr. Perkovic, the milk roundsman who delivered milk to Holy Vale during the relevant years. He said he used to see Stephen almost every day and would often talk to him, and Stephen would often come out to meet him.

"How did he appear in physique to you?" enquired Mr. Elfer.

"A fragile, nervous type of youngster."

"When he came out to meet you, would he talk with you?"

"Oh yes, very often; he used to want to talk to me, discuss something or other."

"And, when his father came on the scene, what happened then?"

"He would just change, or move away; whatever we were talking about; he would stop and that was it."

"And how did he appear to behave towards his father?"

"I would have thought nervous, afraid of him."

Mr. Perkovic told the Jury that on one occasion when he had been delivering milk he had seen Tom Menheniott slap Stephen while they were working on a car. Stephen was handing his father something at which point Menheniott swore at his son and slapped him across the face.

"What effect did it have upon Stephen?" asked Mr. Elfer.

"It put him off balance."

"Was he able to stay on his feet?"

"Yes."

Mr. Field-Fisher in cross-examination, asked Mr. Perkovic to confirm that he would have seen Stephen off and on nearly every day between 1972 and "when he ceased to live there" and must have seen him many hundreds of times?

"I have, yes."

"And you have never seen any sort of mark on his face?"

"Well, I cannot say that I did."

"And on many of these occasions you spoke to him or he spoke to you?"

"Yes. He used to come half way down the drive to meet me and take the milk from me."

69

"And then you would have a few words?"

"Yes."

"And this was in fact the only occasion when you saw any violence?"

"Just once, the only occasion."

"Yes, thank you," said Mr. Field-Fisher, concluding his cross-examination.

The main thrust of the evidence yet to be called was to encompass matters forensic, but before that stage was reached other witnesses gave additional evidence of Menheniott's brutish treatment towards his son, similar to that given upon committal. There was evidence of punches and kicks to Stephen: of tea being thrown over him because it was too hot to drink; of Stephen being seen tethered to a greenhouse for at least forty-five minutes by a rope tied around his waist. A Mrs. Frances Hicks, out riding, saw Menheniott land four punches on Stephen's head.

"He was really punching home and he meant it," she said. Mr. Peakman from Birmingham, a visitor to the islands, recounted how, in July 1975, he had seen Menheniott wielding a piece of timber and then clubbing Stephen to the ground and then kicking him as he lay there. There was also evidence of Stephen walking about in a hunched-up posture and only being able to shuffle about.

Listening to these eye-witness accounts of the violence and cruelty meted out to Stephen, one may be forgiven for asking why no complaints ever reached the police or social services. Should not Elizabeth's children have had visits from social workers, and if that had happened would not, indirectly, Stephen's position have been monitored, as it should have been in any event?

Evidence as to the enquiries made by the police once Stephen's disappearance became known to them, and of the interviews with Menheniott, recited earlier, was presented to the court. Most unusually, this evidence was not disputed in any material respect by the defence - presumably because for most of his interviews with the police Menheniott was accompanied by one or other of his legal advisors.

DAY FOUR

Friday saw the second expert witness begin his evidence. He was Mr. Alexander Davies, a Registered Dental Practitioner and a Consultant Oral Surgeon at Plymouth General Hospital, whose speciality was surgery in relation to the jaws and face. He was handed Stephen's skull, and in answer to questions put to him by Mr. Owen-Thomas confirmed that he had examined it five days after the body had been discovered and that he had found that five teeth in the upper set were missing.

Counsel told Mr. Davies that Mr. Fairest had confirmed that he had extracted three of those teeth on 8th November 1975.

70

"Looking at the places from which those teeth had been drawn," Counsel said, "are you able to say, as a maximum period, how long it takes for a complete restoration of the socket after extraction?"

"Well," said Mr. Davies, "There has been some research carried out in this field which shows that the bone is completely regenerated in a socket at a period of fifteen weeks after extraction of a tooth."

"Looking at the three points of extraction, has the bone been fully regenerated?"

"Not completely."

"Once a patient is dead, does regeneration of the bone continue or does it cease?"

"It ceases."

"So therefore, it would seem to follow from what you have said, that less than fifteen weeks had elapsed from 8th November, the date of extraction, by the time of death?"

"Yes."

Mr. Fairest had fitted a provisional denture in Stephen's mouth, and the question arose as to whether a denture in the mouth could in any way effect the fifteen-week regeneration period.

"Whether or not there is a denture in position, the complete regeneration would take about fifteen weeks?" queried Mr. Owen-Thomas.

"That is correct."

"So, it still follows that it was less than fifteen weeks at the time of death?"

"Yes." replied Mr. Davies.

Counsel now turned to the two teeth found to be missing from the upper set upon exhumation but which had not been extracted by Mr. Fairest. These were the upper right canine and the upper left central incisor, and Mr. Davies confirmed that the canine tooth has the longest root of all teeth and is the most difficult to extract. He further confirmed that the bone in which the upper front teeth are set is called the labial plate and that in this case it was missing over the socket of these two teeth.

Mr. Davies said it would be unusual to lose any of the labial plate when extracting an incisor. In the case of the extraction of a canine tooth some labial plate might come away with the tooth, but not usually to the full depth of the socket.

"And has it in this case," enquired Counsel, "gone to the full depth of the socket?"

"Yes."

"In your view, what sort of force was it that caused the loss of the canine tooth?"

"I think it is most likely that the tooth was displaced inwards."

"Does that mean," continued Mr. Owen-Thomas, "that in doing

71

that, the force could have been sufficient to tear away the labial plate in front of the socket?"

"Yes," Mr. Davies replied.

"From your experience, what sort of force would be necessary to cause that damage?"

"Considerable force. It would require a blow of some force."

"Would a punch in the mouth generate sufficient force?"

"Yes." And in answer to a further question from Counsel, Mr. Davies said that a rabbit punch would also provide the force required and he would, in such circumstances, expect to find damage to the upper lip.

"There is some evidence," Counsel said, "that on the evening before he died, he was struck in the face and his mouth was bleeding. Would that be consistent or inconsistent with the sort of condition one might expect from a blow that had dislodged one or other, or both, of these teeth?"

"It could be consistent, but I cannot give any opinion with reference to the timing of it."

"If the tooth was knocked, or teeth were knocked, out with a blow, would that cause bleeding?"

"Certainly."

"Dealing with the incisor which is gone as well, could that be knocked out in a similar manner?"

"Yes," Mr. Davies replied.

"Would that require as much force as the canine?"

"It would not require as much force."

"And from their spacing, would they be consistent with being knocked out by one blow or would it be more than one blow?"

"They could be knocked out by one blow."

"From the condition of the two sockets, are you able to express a view as to how recent the removal of those teeth had been in relation to the time of death?"

"They had occurred shortly before death," Mr. Davies replied categorically, adding that he could say this as the bony edges of the sockets showed no signs of regeneration and were still sharp.

"I think you were in court when Mr. Fairest was cross-examined," Mr. Owen-Thomas said. "The suggestion was made that these teeth might have been dislodged as a result of somebody tamping down the earth to make the ground firm. What do you say about that?"

"I think it is highly unlikely. It would require a localised force to dislodge these teeth. The effect of the soil covering the face would tend to dissipate this force and if there was a force sufficient to dislodge the teeth then there would be signs of bone injury as well."

"Is there any sign of bone injury other than the local bone injury to which you have referred?"

"No," replied Mr. Davies. The lack of stones at the grave strengthened his opinion that flattening the grave was not a valid explanation for the dislodgement of the two teeth.

"You may remember," Counsel said, "there was a suggestion that perhaps a tractor tyre running over the grave could cause these two teeth to disappear from their positions. What do you say about that?"

"I do not think that is likely. Why should two teeth be dislodged and no other teeth be dislodged? I would have thought that more than the two teeth in question would have been removed. Certainly I would have thought there would have been signs of crush injury."

"Is there any sign of crush injury?"

"Not that I can see," replied Mr. Davies.

Mr. Field-Fisher now rose to cross-examine. Mr. Davies immediately discounted the possibility that a shovel, used at Stephen's burial, could have caused the loss of the two teeth.

Backed up by a report commissioned from a Mr. Sims, a dental expert, Counsel asked Mr. Davies to confirm that the enamel of three of the *lower* teeth was flaking off. Mr. Davies agreed with this, but disagreed with the theory that a fall on the chin could cause the upper and lower jaws to bang together in such a way as to cause the enamel on the lower teeth to fracture, thus precipitating the upper canine out of its socket. However, Mr. Davies, whilst disagreeing with this theory, said that if he had to accept it, the effect would be that the upper right canine tooth in question would be knocked *out* of the mouth, and not *into* the mouth.

"You were told by my Learned friend that there was evidence that there was a blow to the mouth on the night before this boy died. Let us assume," Counsel continued, "that is the position, and you were asked to form some sort of view about whether that might have caused the loss of the two teeth that we know were the last two to be lost. A blow of that nature, sufficient to cause the loss of those two teeth, would cause very severe pain and discomfort, would it not?"

"Yes."

"Very acute?"

"Yes."

"You would have a very sore mouth inside?"

"Yes."

"If the evidence was that the person concerned had been struck in the face and behaved perfectly normally for some considerable time after that, had gone and run himself a bath and had a bath perfectly normally, had not been seen to put his hand to his mouth or anything of that sort, had got himself into his pyjamas, had gone to have another part of his body treated because he had some infection in his leg, would that surprise you in the circumstances?" enquired Mr. Field-Fisher.

"If it had been his first experience, he would be uncomfortable."

73

"He would show it almost invariably?"

"We all have different pain thresholds," replied Mr. Davies. "What one person can stand, another person cannot."

Re-examined by Mr. Owen-Thomas, Mr. Davies said that considerable force would be required to remove the upper canine tooth if it was hit directly and even more force would be needed if it had been dislodged by a blow to the chin, which would have involved the transmission of energy through the lower jaw and teeth into the upper tooth.

"I have no knowledge," prosecuting Counsel said, "as to how this force to the chin occurred as was suggested to you, but I want to try and see whether it could have occurred in a particular way. You know it is the evidence here that this boy, when his foot was up, apparently fell backwards and banged the back of his head on something or other?"

Here, Mr. Field-Fisher interjected to say that he felt it right to say that one defence theory was that Stephen had fallen out of a tree directly onto his chin. Mr. Davies replied that he would be surprised if a symphysio fracture of the mandible (a fracture of the lower jaw) did not result from such an accident, but he found that theory unlikely since the natural instinct would be to cover one's head with one's arms which would protect the jaw.

Mr. Justice Willis interposed at this juncture: "This is a serious matter. If there should have been a force sufficient to damage the teeth, to put it quite simply, by a fall from a tree, it would require the faller to be in a position where he was not protecting himself with his arms at all?"

"His chin would have to make contact with a hard object," replied Mr. Davies.

"And if that were to arise," continued the Judge, "you would certainly find a symphysio fracture of the mandible?"

"Most likely," responded Mr. Davies. He then stood down from the witness box, to be replaced by Dr. A.C. Hunt, a Home Office Pathologist, who had been practising in forensic pathology for some 27 years. A stillness seemed to descend on the court as he entered the witness box, as if everyone knew that vital exchanges were about to take place.

He confirmed to Mr. Owen-Thomas that at 5.30 p.m. on 18th May that year (1977) he had gone with a number of police officers to a corner of California Field at Holy Vale and there had assisted in the removal of broken branches from a particular area. None was large enough to need more than one person to pull them away.

"You were going to dig to see if there was a body there?"

"Yes," replied Dr. Hunt. "All the branches were lying much in the same direction and we therefore decided to excavate down the line of the branches. After some time we came upon some material which later turned out to be the pyjamas the body was wearing," and they then realised that

74

they were indeed excavating a grave. The soil, recalled Dr. Hunt, was white clay having the consistency of wet modelling clay.

"Who removed the soil from around the head?" Counsel enquired.

"I did that myself," replied Dr. Hunt. "Away from the head with a spade and over the face and beside the head with a trowel and a piece of wood to scrape away."

"Did you eventually lay bare the whole of the head?"

"Yes."

"Mr. Fairest was there?"

"Yes."

"Did he then look in the mouth?"

"Yes."

"Did you look first?"

"Yes, I looked first and there were obviously teeth missing and I then asked Mr. Fairest to check with his records."

"And when you looked first were the two teeth with which we are so concerned, the right upper canine and the left incisor, missing?"

"Yes."

"Did you look in the oral cavity to see if there were any objects, including teeth, lying loose, as it were?"

"I did, yes."

"Did you find any?" enquired Counsel.

"No."

"Having regard to the quality of the soil - this clay - if the teeth had become dislodged outward rather than inward once the body was buried, was there any way in your opinion in which they could have strayed away from the area of the face?"

"Oh, no. I think they must have been near the face."

"Were the remains then removed from the grave?"

"They were, yes."

"Did you," asked Counsel, "examine the soil, the clay, upon which the head and surrounding parts had been lying?"

"Yes, the whole of the grave area," replied the pathologist.

"Did you find anything there?"

"No."

"If there had been teeth lying loose in the area where the head had been, would you have found them?"

"Yes. If they had come out of the body during burial, I would have found them." Dr. Hunt also said he would have found them if they had become dislodged in any way after the burial.

"It had got some clothing on it, this body, is that right?" Mr. Owen-Thomas asked.

"Yes, it had."

"What about the body tissue, what most of us would call flesh?"

"This was very badly decomposed, so that most of it had been turned into a sort of fatty wax substance known as adipocere. There was still some skin but completely changed and altered so that one could not recognise any features to it."

"The following day did you carry out a post-mortem examination of the body at the hospital at St. Mary's?" asked Mr. Owen-Thomas.

"I did, yes."

"Was it then wearing a pullover, a waistcoat and a shirt?"

"Yes, it was."

"Pyjama trousers?"

"Yes."

"With the cord tied?"

"The cord was tied around the waist in the ordinary way."

"And some red underpants?"

"Yes."

"What about the internal organs?"

"There were just traces of them, but many of them were missing and one could not form any opinion on them at all," Dr. Hunt replied.

"Did you have the remains x-rayed before the bones were removed?"

"Yes, I had them x-rayed before I opened the body."

"What I want to establish is this," Counsel said. "You know that in your collection of broken ribs one part of the seventh rib is missing?"

"Yes."

"Was that in fact with the body?"

"Yes, that was still with the body. It could not have been lost because the body was completely enclosed in clothing."

"Would you take the skull?" asked Counsel. The skull was handed up to the pathologist and Mr. Owen-Thomas then asked, "What did you find so far as the skull was concerned?"

"First of all I had originally thought there might be a fracture, but when I examined it in the laboratory one could definitely exclude a fracture."

"Was there somewhere on top of the skull an unusual feature?"

"On the left side of the top of the skull there is a straight line of rough bone which is not a normal feature of the skull. It is just over an inch long."

"What is the sort of thing that would cause that condition?" Counsel enquired.

"In my opinion this has been caused by a not particularly severe injury at some time in the past. By the past I mean perhaps up to a number of years ago."

Dr. Hunt then went on to say that his examination of the skull caused him to exclude death having been caused by a head injury by itself.

A cabinet containing a mounted display of Stephen's ribs was now handed to the witness who confirmed that he had found a series of fractures of the ribs. Two of the fractures probably occurred at the same time, as the ribs were adjacent to each other, and Dr. Hunt estimated that these fractures occurred within a time bracket of between a few weeks and a few months before death. One of these ribs had been completely severed whilst the other had also been completely severed but had healed over before death.

"What sort of force is necessary in the case of someone who is 18 or 19, to break the ribs completely through?"

"Quite considerable force. They are springy, and at this age these particular ribs are quite solid ones."

Counsel now referred to another rib, the seventh left, and Dr. Hunt confirmed that this also had been completely severed, and within the same time bracket as the other two, or possibly a little nearer the time of death. He discounted, however, the possibility of all three ribs having been fractured by one and the same blow, as the distance between them was too great.

A fractured right rib, the fourth to be shown to the Jury, was now discussed and Dr. Hunt said that although this one had been fractured within the same time bracket as the other three, it had been fractured more recently than the others. Again, however, it had been completely severed. Dr. Hunt then pointed out that this rib had sustained a second fracture, which had probably occurred between three and seven days before Stephen's death.

"If I may just summarise what we now have," Counsel said. "We have got five fractures, involving at least four separate applications of force?"

"Yes."

"Take, for instance, a fall out of a tree; what do you say about that causing any one of those injuries?"

"I think a fall out of a tree could only cause any of these injuries if the person falling fell on to, for example, a stone sticking up, and of course this could only account for one injury."

"If," enquired Mr. Owen-Thomas, "they were all caused by falls, you would have to have a series of falls out of a series of trees, or the same tree."

"More than that," stated Dr. Hunt. "You would have to have a series of falls and each time he would have had to have landed on a projecting stone."

"You have heard," Counsel stated, "that on one occasion Stephen was struck across the back with a piece of tubular scaffold with sufficient force to fell him. Would that be consistent with causing the sort of injuries that you found there?"

"Oh, yes," responded Dr. Hunt. "To fell someone with a blow of that nature would have to be severe, very severe, and would be just the sort of force that might have produced any one of those fractures."

"Then we heard about a blow with a shovel; would that be the sort of force that would be consistent with causing one of the injuries you found?"

"Yes, any one," replied Dr. Hunt.

Dr. Hunt was not certain, owing to its lightness of weight, whether the broomstick could have caused any of the fractures, but said it was possible if the head was on the broom and the head made contact with the ribs. A blow with a piece of timber followed by a kick would also be the sort of application of force which might result in a fractured rib.

"What effect would you expect these fractures to have, however they were caused, upon the comfort or otherwise of the person to whom they were caused?" asked Mr. Owen-Thomas.

"They would cause him a great deal of pain from the broken ends rubbing together. The pain of a fractured rib is quite severe usually."

"What would you expect to follow from a person who has sustained injuries of this sort?"

"I presume one would expect him to make a lot of fuss; an ordinary person would make a lot of fuss and seek medical attention straight away."

Dr. Hunt then went on to explain that ribs fractured in the way Stephen's had been, could puncture the membrane over the lung and enter the lung itself. This might have caused pneumonia, particularly as no medical treatment was offered. Pneumonia would be more likely if Stephen had injuries to his mouth, because it is well known that in such circumstances one inhales blood and the combination of mouth injury and rib injury is particularly liable to produce a chest infection. The consequence of this would be that the patient would become increasingly ill over a matter of a couple of days and could succumb to his pneumonia.

Dr. Hunt believed that if Stephen had been struck in the manner previously outlined on the night he died, and the ribs had previously been fractured but had not punctured the lung, the injuries sustained on that last night could themselves have caused the lung to puncture. Such a chain of events could have caused a quick death since it would cause bleeding into the cavity around the lung with the result that air might get into that cavity causing the lung to collapse. The effect of this would be that the patient dies of lack of oxygen in his blood system, or air starvation, in effect suffocation.

In the light of his post-mortem findings, and in particular the fact that the skull was not fractured, Dr. Hunt ruled out the possibility of Stephen dying of a head injury as such, a crucial opinion in view of defence evidence yet to be called, but believed that head injuries added to the other factors might have had a cumulative effect which brought about death.

Mr. Owen-Thomas referred to evidence previously given of Stephen lying in his room and moaning and groaning on the night of his death, and asked Dr. Hunt what degree of discomfort the boy would have been in, based on the theory of a punctured lung.

"It would be severe," replied Dr. Hunt. "He could well have been moaning because of the pain from his ribs and the fact that he could not breathe properly."

"If he were lying on the ground in that way, and if his mouth were bleeding, would that have any relevance?" Counsel enquired.

"Yes, it could well do. If he is partly unconscious for lack of oxygen or chest infection, he is much more likely to inhale blood from an injured mouth, and this would add to his chances of not surviving."

Mr. Owen-Thomas asked: "If you had someone who is subjected to a course of conduct over a period of time, assuming it to be a fact that he was struck with a number of objects resulting in these fractured ribs during the last six months of his life, and then he dies, what do you say is the conjunction between death and those actions?"

"It would be beyond reasonable possibility that they were not the cause of death," replied Dr. Hunt.

DAY FIVE

At this stage the Court adjourned for the weekend. The prosecution case appeared to have gone well so far, and as the Jury dispersed to homes all over the county, one wondered what provisional views they were forming as to Menheniott's culpability. The court reconvened at 10.30 a.m. on Monday, 12th December with Dr. Hunt preparing himself for cross-examination by Mr. Field-Fisher, Q.C.

"It comes to this, does it not," stated Counsel, "that you are unable to say positively what was the cause of death. From the careful examination that one knows was made, you are quite unable to say 'This was in my definite opinion the cause of death'?"

Dr. Hunt agreed that he could not specify an exact cause of death and also agreed that he had had to speculate as to the cause of death owing to the state of the body upon exhumation.

Dr. Hunt said that his examination of the body showed that Stephen had a congenital deformity at the top end of the spine. Counsel agreed, saying that there was evidence that Stephen always had a poor posture with an exaggerated spinal curvature, and put to Dr. Hunt that this condition "would be completely consistent with the description that you have heard from one or two witnesses of seeing him in this hunched position, shuffling about."

"Yes, if there was evidence that this was the way he always walked, quite," replied the pathologist, explaining that there could be other reasons for the boy's posture.

79

Counsel now turned to the exhumation of Stephen's body and obtained agreement from Dr. Hunt that he had not thought of specifically looking for the two missing teeth after Mr. Fairest had pointed out to him that they were in fact missing from the skull. He said he had removed the soil very carefully and would not have missed the teeth. He also denied Counsel's suggestion that the fracture of the rib which had been fractured in two places could have occurred after death. The second fracture of that rib would have occurred within three to seven days before death.

Under further questioning, however, Dr. Hunt had to agree that it was a possibility that certain of the rib fractures could have occurred after death when the body was being dressed and then carted to its resting place in the wheelbarrow. This somewhat surprising admission goes some way to show how difficult it must be to formulate definite opinions when an examination of the remains necessarily has to take place so long after death.

"One of the outstanding pieces of evidence, I suggest to you," said Mr. Field-Fisher, "and you can agree or disagree with this is, when one comes to consider the events of the last night, Elizabeth's evidence that the deceased was in all ways perfectly normal in health and behaviour up until the time he went into his father's bedroom?"

"I found it very remarkable."

"Now that must mean, and that is the only evidence we have of his actual state of health on that night, that there could not have been complications such as you name which had already developed by that night?"

"My feeling was that this evidence may not in fact be reliable," retorted Dr. Hunt, "inasmuch as it may be quite difficult to tell whether someone is ill, and having been to the house and seen the sort of state in which these people lived, she might not have recognised the fact."

"I follow that," Counsel said, "but the fact is it is the only evidence we have, and if her evidence be correct, at any rate he had a bath, he undressed himself to have the bath, he managed perfectly well in the bath, he got out and put his pyjamas on, he went up the stairs, he went to his father's room for the purpose of having his leg dressed. That would suggest a state of normality, would it not?"

"Yes," replied Dr. Hunt. "One of the remarkable things in this case is that he has all these fractures which with a normal person you would think would be causing a great deal of trouble and we do not have any evidence from his family that he was ill."

"It goes further than that, I think," Counsel said, "because so far as the earlier fractures are concerned there was evidence from Mr. Fairest that at the end of November he appeared to be in, for him, perfectly normal health?"

"Yes, yes, very odd."

"So we have him in perfectly normal health, so far as Mr. Fairest is concerned, at the end of November. We have no evidence from other members of the family who gave evidence about Boxing Day events, that he was in anything except normal health. That is right, is it not?" asked Counsel.

"Quite. He was in a normal state," Dr. Hunt replied, "but whether that was a healthy state or not is another matter." He went on to say that it was this apparent normality that led him to believe that the most likely cause of death was the most recently fractured rib banging into Stephen's lung on that last evening when he fell, "and that it was damage to the lung which killed him."

"If he had developed pneumonia at any time within the seven days before that last night," Mr. Field-Fisher asked, "he would have been very ill on the last night, before ever the rabbit punching incident arose?"

"Yes," replied Dr. Hunt, "I think he would be obviously ill. He would have had a temperature."

Dr. Hunt agreed that Stephen's coldness, as when Elizabeth found her brother lying on his bedroom floor, was consistent with shock, but was not inconsistent with an earlier temperature.

"Now," said Counsel, "I put to you the unlikelihood of this boy, on the evidence that we have got, suffering from any sort of pneumonia or similar complication up until the time of the rabbit punch?"

"Yes, if one accepts Mrs. Rayner's evidence."

Mr. Field-Fisher then asked for confirmation that what Dr. Hunt was putting forward as one theory was that the rabbit punches on the last night had caused a rib, the fifth injury, to fracture and pierce the lung.

"Yes," replied Dr. Hunt. "I was putting it forward as a possibility - that it had been fractured a couple of days before, and the rabbit-punching then pushed it through."

Counsel then asked: "And he would quickly become very ill within a few hours, probably within minutes?"

"Yes, he probably would."

Mr. Field-Fisher, following Dr. Hunt's line of thought through, said that if Stephen was suffering in the way envisaged, it seemed very unlikely that he would then have run himself a bath, and taken all the other actions shown by the evidence, and then gone into his father's room, and this a fairly considerable time after the rabbit-punching incident. Dr. Hunt could do nothing but agree, and said that he certainly thought Stephen would "want to go and lie down."

Mr. Field-Fisher now turned his attentions to a defence theory relating to the cause of death. "You know Dr. Hocking, sitting behind me, very well. He will be giving evidence about this matter and his belief is, and I must put it to you, that the cause of death was directly related to the blow to the head he suffered in the bedroom. You have said that you would not expect any severe injury from the distance involved, and you would have expected a fracture of the skull if the blow had been enough to cause death. By that you meant, of course, directly causing death?"

"Yes," Dr. Hunt replied.

Counsel now put to Dr. Hunt the facts as given to the court by Mrs. Rayner of the incident in her father's bedroom, of Stephen falling over and banging the back of his head on the wall during the leg-bandaging session, of him then crawling out of the room, of later hearing him moaning and mumbling. "Now," asked Counsel, "is that description consistent with somebody who is suffering a form of concussion in some degree or another?"

"No, not entirely, because by definition concussion means that the patient has become completely unconscious."

"From those few facts," insisted Counsel, "it would be perfectly possible for him to have suffered from momentary loss of full consciousness and thereafter be in a semi-conscious state?"

"Yes, if one had in fact been knocked out, I would accept that he could then he concussed," agreed Dr. Hunt.

"Loss of consciousness could be as little as just a few seconds, could it not?"

"Yes," Dr. Hunt replied.

"Is it possible there might be a full momentary loss of consciousness followed by a more prolonged period of mussiness later?"

"Yes."

"That would be consistent with his mumbling and being unintelligible at a later stage?"

"Yes," replied Dr. Hunt, but he went on to say that Stephen's behaviour, though consistent with post-concussional effect, was in his opinion unlikely to have been caused by it.

"Would you tell us why," enquired Mr. Field-Fisher.

"Because for him to have been as semi-conscious as that for so long, I would have expected him to have received a severe enough head injury to have at least produced a slight fracture of the skull."

Mr. Justice Willis: "Wait a minute. So far as the period of time is concerned, I have assumed that it is six hours, 9.00 p.m. to 3.00 a.m.?"

"Yes, my Lord," replied Mr. Field-Fisher, "I think the evidence is that these general events started about 9.00 p.m."

At this stage the court adjourned for a short while, and when the proceedings re-commenced Mr. Field-Fisher asked Dr. Hunt: "Before the adjournment we were examining the possibility of concussion. I stress that there is no suggestion that the blow on the head directly killed him."

"Quite."

"There has to be the introduction of some other agency to bring about death."

82

"Yes."

"I think you assumed one of the possibilities would be bleeding?"

"Yes."

"In a semi-conscious state, bleeding from the mouth, eventually leading to suffocation?"

"Yes."

"Now one of the signs of that would be increasing respiratory trouble, would it not?"

"Yes."

"There is no evidence of that, is there?"

"No." Dr. Hunt continued by admitting that he was only speculating, but one of the possibilities he could not exclude was that Stephen drowned in his own blood. But Mr. Field-Fisher put to Dr. Hunt that one of the outstanding possibilities was that Stephen died of suffocation, either by rolling "onto his face on the bed and suffocating in the pillow" or through "inhalation of vomit" or by swallowing his own tongue. After some prevarication, Dr. Hunt agreed that he "could not exclude suffocation from my finding." He made it clear, however, that he only considered suffocation to be a remote possibility as the cause of Stephen's death. He also discounted the possibility of Stephen having died from natural causes. "It is a very remote posssibility, a coincidence I would find unacceptable."

Counsel asked: "The heart was not preserved?"

"Oh, no."

"So you are not really able to say anything about the condition of the heart?"

"No. There are one or two rare heart diseases which do cause sudden death in this age group."

"It is perfectly possible, but you are taking the view that it is very unlikely?"

"Exactly."

Counsel now turned to another aspect of the case; the breaking of Stephen's ribs. Dr. Hunt agreed that the assault that Mr. Peakman from Birmingham witnessed in July 1975 would not have caused the first fractures. They would have occurred later. Counsel also suggested that it was not beyond the realms of possibility that the rib and teeth injuries could have been caused by a fall from a tree, particularly if the fall might have taken Stephen through projecting branches. Dr. Hunt did not think much of that possibility, particularly in relation to the rib which had suffered two fractures: "I cannot envisage one falling through a tree and bouncing onto different branches and breaking a rib twice in two different places." It was really the multiplicity of injuries which made him reject such a theory.

Counsel said: "There were various pieces of evidence, and the Jury will remember I am sure, about the boy shielding himself from time to time with his hands; do you remember?"

"Yes."

"From blows. There was no evidence was there, of any injuries to his hands or wrists of any sort?"

"No. There were no fractured bones. In quite serious attacks in which a patient shields himself you may get quite bad injuries but the bones do not fracture."

"Not necessarily; but again it is not unknown?" asked Counsel.

"One occasionally sees fractured hands."

"There was no evidence whatsoever of that?"

"No."

"It is possible, is it not, that the last fracture we are talking about, within his last three to seven days, could have been caused by falling against furniture, a table or a chair?"

"Yes, if the body hit the furniture with sufficient force."

"It is not," Counsel enquired, "unknown for that type of injury to take place in the home?"

"In old people it is not infrequent, but in a youth with bones like this, which are really quite normal bones, at his age, it has to hit the furniture with quite considerable force."

"Lastly, there is a good deal of evidence that the Crown rely upon relating to blows to this boy's face?"

"Yes."

"If that had been the sort of pattern of events, one of the things most at risk is the face and the nose, is it not?"

"Yes."

"There was no evidence of any fracture of the nose?"

"No."

Dr. Hunt's re-examination by Mr. Owen-Thomas concentrated on tightening up, and clarifying for the Jury's benefit, various aspects of his evidence: no, he would not expect to find bony injuries to the hands caused by punches; and whether punches to the face might cause a broken nose would depend upon where the blows landed. It was unlikely, he felt, that any of Stephen's injuries had been caused by him falling from the tree which had the block and tackle attached to it. This tree was near the flower packing sheds, which were some 200 yards from the cottage. The height of the branch with the block and tackle was fifteen feet, three inches, from the ground, an exact measurement as "Sergeant Robinson climbed the tree in my presence and suspended a tape measure and I measured the bottom of it." Dr. Hunt felt that Stephen would have had to have been a further ten feet above the block and tackle, that is twenty-five feet from the ground, if he was to hit the block and tackle or an adjacent stub with sufficient momentum to cause the rib fractures. Dr. Hunt explained to the Jury that in such circumstances Stephen could easily have broken an arm or a leg, but no such fractures were found.

Dr. Hunt emphasised, in answer to further questions from Mr. Owen-Thomas, that had Stephen's missing teeth been dislodged during the act of burial or whilst the grave was being covered he would certainly have found them during his excavations at the time of the exhumation.

Shortly after these exchanges, Dr. Hunt left the witness box and Mr. Owen-Thomas, addressing Mr. Justice Willis, said: "My Lord, that is the case for the Crown."

Mr. Field-Fisher, rising, said: "My Lord, I have some observations to make and I think they would perhaps best be made in the absence of the Jury."

Mr. Justice Willis: "Very well. Would you mind retiring, Members of the Jury."

After they had withdrawn, Mr. Field-Fisher said: "My Lord, so far as murder is concerned, one has to start, in my submission, with a high degree of certainty about the cause of death. The position here is that Dr. Hunt, with the evidence available, has formulated certain propositions. He is transparently honest in saying that it is impossible to be precise about this matter, and it seems to me that we are in a situation where he has formulated certain possibilities and he has favoured one perhaps more than another. He has examined all the material that is available to him and he is not, at the end, able to say that the cause of death would be 'this or that' with any degree of certainty at all."

"Dr. Hunt is simply theorising. He, of course, is fully entitled to theorise. That is one of the things he has to do, but then one has to put into the balance the other possibilities I have put to him."

"I put to Dr. Hunt various possibilities. He felt that it was very unlikely that Stephen suffocated on his pillow. The second possibility was that there was an inhalation of vomit, and he agreed. He said, 'Yes that is a possibility which cannot be excluded.' "

"Then there is this, My Lord: So far as murder is concerned, the prosecution must prove either that he intended to kill......"

Mr. Justice Willis intervened: "They are not relying on that, are they?"

"No, my Lord," Mr. Field-Fisher replied. "Or that he inflicted injury with intent to do some really serious harm. Now, my Lord, we are back to the rabbit punch which, it seems to me, has now become the bedrock of the Prosecution's case as to what happened on the last night. Can it really be said that if somebody inflicts a rabbit punch on the back of his son that he intended at that time to cause really serious injury?"

Mr. Justice Willis asked, "Is it not really a matter for the Jury?"

"If your Lordship takes that view, I will not take up more of your

Lordship's time. But I would invite your Lordship's attention to the events which then proceeded, by the boy going along to have his leg dressed by his father; it does not seem to me that a good father, who is treating his boy's leg in that way, would be ill-treating him. He is treating him obviously in a humane way. How can it be said that a father who was doing that for the boy intended to cause really serious harm? That is how I put that submission to your Lordship."

Mr. Justice Willis: "What have you got to say in reply to Mr. Field-Fisher's submissions, Mr. Owen-Thomas? I do not think you need trouble about the question of intent. I think that is a matter for the Jury."

Mr. Owen-Thomas: "This is, in effect, the type of case where you do not have a body. It is open to the Jury, having heard all the evidence, to infer that the cause of death was the result of the injuries inflicted by the accused."

"It is open to the Jury, having heard about the scaffold pole, the shovel, the injury to the teeth and the broomstick, to consider such conduct, which is plainly of a debilitating type. If, during a course of such action, you render a person into that sort of condition then, my Lord, one has to take one's victim as you find him. If you then engage in a further unlawful act which accelerates his death then that, my Lord, produces an unlawful killing."

"The authority for that is to be found in R.v. Dyson which is reported in Volume 2, 1908 King's Bench Division at page 454. The headnote reads, 'On the trial of an indictment for manslaughter there was evidence that the prisoner had inflicted injuries upon the deceased more than a year and a day before the date of the death, and also certain further injuries within that period which tended to accelerate death.' The point of my submission is to be found in the Judgement of Lord Alverstone, Lord Chief Justice. It is a very short Judgement. May I read it to your Lordship?"

"Judgments always were in those days," remarked the Judge.

Mr. Owen-Thomas, reading from the report: 'The prisoner was indicted for the manslaughter of his child, who died on March 5th, 1908. There was evidence that the prisoner had inflicted injuries upon the child in November, 1906 and certain further injuries in December, 1907. The jury convicted the prisoner, who appeals against that conviction upon the ground that the judge misdirected the jury in that he left it to them to find the prisoner guilty if they considered the death to have been caused by the injuries inflicted in 1906. This was clearly not a proper direction, for, whatever one may think of the merits of such a rule of law, it is still undoubtedly the law of the land that no person can be convicted of manslaughter where the death does not occur within a year and a day after the injury was inflicted, for in that event it must be attributed to some other cause. Under these circumstances, there having been a mis-direction, the

question arises whether the Court can nevertheless dismiss the appeal.'
'The proper question to have been submitted to the jury was whether the prisoner accelerated the child's death by the injuries which he inflicted in December, 1907. For if he did, the fact that the child was already suffering from meningitis, from which it would in any event have died before long, would afford no answer to the charge of causing its death. If that question had been left to the jury, they would in all probability have found the prisoner guilty on*the ground', and so it goes on.

"That being so, my Lord," Mr. Owen-Thomas continued, "if you wreck somebody's health and reduce them to a pitiable physical state, and then you unlawfully perpetrate the *coup de grâce* which accelerates death, that becomes unlawful killing."

"I want to be quite sure that I understand you correctly," Mr. Justice Willis said. "The Jury have got to consider here, if they dismiss natural causes as a cause of death, whether they are sure they can exclude accident, and before there can be a conviction of either murder or manslaughter, they have got to be sure that death was caused by an injury inflicted by the accused man?"

"Yes, my Lord."

Mr. Justice Willis: "Is it sufficient to leave to them, as it were, the general proposition that although they could not positively identify the isolated particular act of violence which caused death, if they were satisfied there had been a cumulative course of conduct which so debilitated the boy and ultimately he died due to injuries inflicted by this man, this would be sufficient for them to convict either of murder or manslaughter, depending upon whether they were satisfied on the question of intent?"

"Yes, my Lord," Mr. Owen-Thomas replied, "I do submit that. Murder is committed if violence is caused to another with the intention of causing death or alternatively grievous bodily harm. In the present case the Crown were not putting their case on the basis of an intention to kill, merely of an intention to commit grievous bodily harm. It is clear, therefore, that if the Jury decided that Menheniott intended to cause Stephen grievous bodily harm on, for instance, the final night and he later died that would amount to murder. If, however, the Jury found no such intent proved, Stephen's subsequent death would amount only to manslaughter."

After hearing further submissions by both Counsel, Mr. Justice Willis gave his ruling, which was short and to the point: "I think this matter should go to the Jury. Let us have the Jury back."

There was then a short pause in the proceedings whilst the Jury returned to Court from their first floor Jury room. As soon as they had settled back in the jury box Mr Field-Fisher opened the Case for the Defence by immediately announcing that Menheniott would not be going into the witness box.

Every accused man in a criminal trial has the right to stay silent. This logically follows on from the basic tenet of criminal law that the prosecution have to prove their case so that the jury are sure of the defendant's guilt. In that task, it is not part of an accused person's duty to assist the prosecution by opening himself to cross-examination. One often wonders, however, as in this case, whether entering the witness box is a risk which simply has to be taken. Human nature being what it is, most juries will have their own views on a defendant's silence, notwithstanding such a right being reinforced by comments of the judge in his summing-up. The defence, however, were clearly relying on the Prosecution's inability to give a definite cause of death, and felt that that would be sufficient to obtain an acquittal on the murder charge.

The first witness for the Defence was Dr. Frederick Hocking. Dr. Hocking is a well-known and respected pathologist in Cornwall, and he confirmed to the court that he was the Cornwall County Pathologist, a position he had held for forty-three years, and that before then he had been a pathologist in London for nine years.

"So far as Dr. Hunt's findings of fact are concerned, do you accept his findings?" asked Mr. Field-Fisher.

"I accept his findings," replied Dr. Hocking.

"I think you have conflict upon what may be deduced from those findings?"

"I do."

"Now, first of all, I want to ask you this. I think you have heard the evidence in this case?"

"I think I have heard it all."

"So far as the events leading up to the death on the last night are concerned, the evidence is that he was found dead at about 3.00 a.m. What," asked Mr. Field-Fisher, "did you find the most single significant factor of Elizabeth's evidence?"

"It was," Dr. Hocking replied, "that Stephen appeared to be in a perfectly normal state of health up to the time he went to have his legs dressed."

Mr. Field-Fisher: "One of the findings that Dr. Hunt made is the finding that the fracture of the seventh rib was shortly before death - that this had been done seven days before death?"

"I agree," replied the rugged Cornish pathologist, will-o'-the-wisp hair characteristically jutting out in the direction of the Jury.

"You agree?"

"Yes."

Dr. Hocking then went through the various medical possibilities flowing from the fracture of the rib which had occurred in those few days before death. He discounted an air embolism caused through the rib tearing into the lung, since that would have caused death within one hour or so of the injury occuring, which clearly was not the position in Stephen's case.

Bearing in mind Stephen's actions on the last night, Dr. Hocking also ruled out air from the lung getting into the cavity between the lung itself and the chest wall so as to cause a collapsed lung. Stephen in such circumstances would have been showing very obvious distress by the last night.

"Again," said Mr. Field-Fisher, "I am dealing with the situation according to Dr. Hunt. He was saying that this particular rib we are talking of was broken three to seven days before death. If you accept that, and the lung immediately collapsed, do you think that by the night of his death he would have been very ill?"

"He would have been very ill; he would have been increasingly ill from the time that the lung was punctured."

"Do you say that the illness would show or not?"

"Very obvious, because of the respiratory distress with the collapsed lung."

"Would he in any way, if he was suffering like that, be able to behave normally about the house?"

"I would think not," replied Dr. Hocking.

"How would he feel?"

"Very ill," was the firm reply.

"Now having regard to the evidence that you have heard, about how he appeared and what he did on the last night, do you think that this is a possibility in this case?"

"I do not think the lung could have been punctured at the time when the fracture occurred."

Dr. Hocking also excluded, as a cause of death, the fracture causing blood to enter the cavity between the lung and the chest wall. Here again, Stephen would have been very ill from the outset, and clearly he was not, since "he was behaving perfectly normally up to the time when he went to have his legs dressed."

"The suggestion has been made," stated Counsel, "that he might have developed pneumonia. Is that another possibility?"

"I think pneumonia is quite out," replied Dr. Hocking. "He would have been very ill indeed, and he would have been running a high temperature. He would have had respiratory distress which would have been very obvious to everybody, laboured breathing and that sort of thing."

"Is there any evidence here of increasing difficulties in his breathing?"

"I think not," replied Dr. Hocking.

"Now those are the possibilities, are they, if he had his lung punctured, or injured through puncturing?"

89

"They are, yes."

"In the circumstances of this case, do you exclude that?"

"I exclude it, yes."

"Now," Mr. Field-Fisher continued, "we come to the night itself. We have had the evidence of Elizabeth, and I hope I am putting it as fairly as possible, and her evidence is that there was an incident in the passage downstairs?"

"Yes."

"Upon Stephen, by the Defendant, one of which was in the mouth, and the other in the back. Two different forms of assaults. She said there was a blow in the mouth from the father. I think there is no reference by her to teeth being knocked out. And the other thing was rabbit punches in the middle of the back."

"Yes."

"The evidence is that Stephen was on the ground for a short time, for five minutes or something like that," stated Mr. Field-Fisher, "and that he then got up and went and had a bath, which he took by himself. Which would mean doing all the things necessary, such as undressing, washing himself, and drying himself, then getting into pyjamas and so on. Does that sound to you like a picture of a boy who had just received a really serious injury?"

"It does not," replied the pathologist.

"Again, we know that he then goes into the father's bedroom to have his leg dressed. Supposing he had had this very serious injury on that last night, what is the first thing people normally feel like doing when they are feeling really ill?"

"Lying down."

"Does it sound likely that he would have gone in to have a relatively trivial matter attended to?"

"No."

"He had to stand on one leg while the other was attended to. Does that sound like someone who was feeling very bad?"

"It does not."

"Then he, according to Elizabeth, had this fall, and you heard her evidence about that," Counsel continued. "Now will you tell the Jury what you think of the sequence of events that happened thereafter?"

"I think that this boy had a fairly, not intensely, severe bang on the head, and falling through a distance of four feet is quite a fall, and would give a fair bang on the head, not enough to fracture the skull as we know the skull was not broken," replied Dr. Hocking.

"We have heard, according to Elizabeth, the situation where she went in to see Stephen. He was confused, mumbling and she couldn't quite understand him, and so on. What does that suggest to you?" Counsel enquired.

"It suggests a partial unconsciousness as a result of the blow on the head. It fits the picture exactly."

As to Stephen being found naked on the floor, Dr. Hocking said that one could only hazard a guess, and that possibly in his confused state he thought that he was undressing himself. As to why he crawled from his father's bedroom on hands and knees, Dr. Hocking's opinion was that he was so knocked out by the blow that he could not get up because of dizziness.

"Elizabeth went in later, and we know she went in several times, and on one occasion she went in and found him noticeably cold. Do you draw any sort of inference from that?" Counsel said.

"That," replied Dr. Hocking, "would be consistent with a condition of shock, shock from the blow to the head."

"Is that noticeably cold reaction of the body consistent with a condition of pneumonia or any of these other matters that we were discussing?" asked Counsel.

"If he had had pneumonia, I am quite sure he would have had heavy sweating and gasping for breath."

At this moment Mr. Justice Willis intervened: "I think this will be a convenient moment to adjourn." The Judge bowed to Counsel and withdrew. Counsel collected up their papers, and the prison officers took Menheniott down to the cells, from where later, as usual, he would be taken to Exeter Prison for the night.

DAY SIX

The following day, Tuesday, 13th December, Mr. Field-Fisher resumed his examination-in-chief of Dr. Hocking.

"On the available evidence, and I stress that observation, what is your view of the most likely way that this boy died?"

"A complication resulting from concussion, the concussion being due to the blow on the head," Dr. Hocking replied. The pathologist went on to explain that one of the possible complications that could arise from such a concussion was that Stephen became rather restless whilst lying on his bed, turned over and suffocated. He felt, however, that that was a remote possibility which could nevertheless have occurred. Another possibility was that Stephen vomited and inhaled his vomit. He explained that if a person partially suffocates whilst semi-conscious or unconscious it is quite common for vomiting to occur due to lack of oxygen to the brain. In such a scenario Stephen would have died within minutes and only a small amount of vomit would have been required. A further possibility was that Stephen choked as a result of his tongue falling back in his mouth. As a possibility, Dr. Hocking placed that on a par with the vomiting theory.

Mr. Field-Fisher said that Dr. Hunt's view of the rabbit punching incident was that it might have caused, or opened up, a fracture of the rib which could have led to death later on the same night, but that this would depend upon the rib puncturing the lung or the membrane round the lung.

"How common," he asked Dr. Hocking, "is it for a broken rib to do just that?"

"In my experience, it is very rare for a single broken rib to penetrate the lung. I have never seen it," replied Dr. Hocking.

Now, turning to the scaffold pole incident, Counsel next asked Dr. Hocking whether if the scaffold pole had been applied in the way that Elizabeth Rayner appeared to suggest, a one-handed blow right across the back, what would he have expected to happen?

"I would expect the blow to have fallen upon the scapula, or perhaps both of the scapulae, and I do not think the ribs underneath would have been fractured," Dr. Hocking replied. "They are protected by a fairly thick layer of muscle around the scapulae. If ribs were fractured it would have been an extremely heavy blow that would also have completely shattered the scapulae."

"What do you say about the blow with the shovel described by Elizabeth?"

"This would be a possible cause of fractured ribs if the blow fell in a precise way. That would be downwards, so that the blade of the shovel just went between the edge of the scapula and the backbone. It could have fractured two ribs, but I should have thought it was more likely to have fractured one only."

"We have heard a great deal in this case from witnesses about blows over the course of the years to Stephen's face," Counsel stated. "Where you have heavy blows, do you generally get heavy bruising?"

"You do."

"How long may heavy bruising last?"

"It could be visible for up to a fortnight or even more."

"Secondly, if you had fairly persistent heavy blows to the face of this boy, would you or would you not expect any bony damage to the face?"

"I would have expected his nose to have been broken on more than one occasion."

"Could the fractures of the fifth and sixth upper ribs have been caused by a fall from a tree?"

"They could if he fell backwards on to a projection - a branch, a stone."

Finally, Mr. Field-Fisher asked Dr. Hocking whether, as suggested by Dr. Hunt, more than one projection would have been required.

"Not necessarily. One fall on to a projection covering the area of two ribs would be sufficient," he replied.

Mr. Owen-Thomas rose to cross-examine, and asked the usher to hand the box containing Stephen's ribs to Dr. Hocking.

"Do you agree that those ribs reveal five fractures, caused on at least four separate occasions within a period of between two to three months up to very nearly the time of death?"

"I do."

"A fractured rib causes considerable pain, made worse by movement?"

"It does." Dr. Hocking also agreed that some of the fractures would have over-lapped with each other.

"Therefore it must have been that either he was able to conceal the pain or that the others did not notice?" said Counsel.

"That is so, yes."

Counsel then proceeded to go into detail on the type and position of the rib injuries, and elicited admissions from Dr. Hocking that in certain circumstances the scaffolding pipe and the shovel could have caused certain of the fractures.

Dr. Hocking also agreed that if Stephen had fractured any ribs by falling from the block and tackle tree, his fall must have commenced some six to ten feet above the projection which caused the injury in order for sufficient momentum to be gained. Alternatively he could have fallen from a mere ten feet up the tree onto a projection on the ground.

"Of course, Dr. Hocking, we are putting these various hypotheses forward because nobody has said how he fell, if, indeed, he ever did fall. Do you follow?"

"I do, yes."

"Now I want to come back to the injury to the rib on the last night. You have to rely very considerably for the opinion that you express upon the description of the conduct of the deceased given by Elizabeth?"

"I do, yes."

"You told us that you relied upon her evidence that Stephen appeared in a perfectly normal state of health up to the time that his legs were dressed?"

Dr. Hocking replied that he relied on that entirely.

"Do you agree that if somebody does have a fracture, and you bump into something as you are going around the house, it will give you, if I might be forgiven for putting it this way, absolute hell?"

"It would do," replied Dr. Hocking.

"The last night, Elizabeth told the Jury that this youth was rabbit punched a number of times to the back. With that sort of chopping motion you get very great force distributed, do you not?"

"Of course."

"The accused man has very large hands, has he not?" Counsel suggested.

"Yes."

"Any blow of that nature would have a very agonising effect,

93

whether it lands on the fracture or not - it will exacerbate existing great pain?"

"Yes."

"Do you agree that in Stephen collapsing to the ground, that is going to cause the rib cage to move?"

"Yes."

Counsel stated that "it would be quite impossible, would it not, to describe this boy as appearing in a normal state of health, if that means somebody is normally in good health?"

"This boy's normal condition was that he had got used to it," was the rather enigmatic reply.

"This is not the picture," Mr. Owen-Thomas insisted, "of somebody who is in good health, is it?"

"It is not, no."

"So you begin by forming your opinion that Stephen was in a perfectly normal state of health?"

"For him," replied the pathologist.

"Oh come, Dr. Hocking. Are you inviting the Jury to come to the conclusion that this youth had become so inured to pain and to disability, that he is to be regarded as being in a normal state of health for him?"

"I think so," was Dr. Hocking's somewhat weak reply.

"Are you content for the worth of your evidence as a whole to be judged upon that answer?"

"Yes."

"Incidentally, you told the Jury yesterday that you were Cornwall County Pathologist. You told us you held that appointment?"

"I did."

"When were you first appointed to that position?"

"In 1934."

"And you were retired in 1964?"

"From the hospital," replied Dr. Hocking.

"There is," stressed Counsel, "no such position as Cornwall County Pathologist?"

"There is, because I hold it," Dr. Hocking replied firmly.

"Elizabeth suffered a stroke in 1977. Would you just explain to the Jury what a stroke involves?"

"It involves destruction of part of the brain either as a result of bleeding into the brain or as a result of cutting off the blood supply to a portion of the brain," explained Dr. Hocking.

"And that will adversely affect a person's memory for detail of events?"

"It might do, depending on the site of the bleeding."

"And of course hers is the only evidence upon which you can rely in giving your conclusions?"

"Yes," replied the doctor.

After further questioning of this witness on matters of medical detail, Counsel asked Dr. Hocking: "You did not see Mrs. Rayner until after her illness?"

"No, but it appeared that she was a perfectly normal person mentally."

"Are you saying," Counsel countered, "that when you saw her here giving evidence she appeared to you to be a perfectly ordinary person mentally?"

"Mentally for her class, shall we say."

Counsel then passed on to Elizabeth's rather hesitant account of the leg-bandaging incident in her father's bedroom and of Stephen falling over.

"If there never was any fall, then any sort of theory about any sort of injury to the head immediately goes?"

"It does."

"Do you agree that the distance through which he could fall backwards is pretty restricted?"

"About four feet it would be," Dr. Hocking replied.

"Now I want to put this to you," Mr. Owen-Thomas said. "Have you ever seen a case of a boy of eighteen or nineteen who has fallen only four feet, not had the slightest fracture of his skull, not cut his head, not had a sizeable haemorrhage inside the skull, has fractured ribs, who has died within six hours after a minor head injury, because of the head injury?"

"No, this is the first case of that type I have ever come across."

"Now how long did you tell the Jury you had been a pathologist?"

"Fifty-odd years."

Soon after this exchange, Mr. Owen-Thomas ended his somewhat telling cross-examination and sank back onto his seat.

After the luncheon adjournment Mr. Field-Fisher rose to ask Dr. Hocking a few additional questions by way of re-examination.

"Have you ever known a case where a young man, who was going to die from a punctured lung and the complications arising from it after five or six hours, behave in the way the evidence suggested that this boy had?"

"No," replied the doctor.

"If this boy's mouth was severely damaged on the night of his death and it continued to bleed substantially thereafter, would you have expected there to have been evidence of a substantial amount or some blood, on the pillow?"

"There would have been, yes."

This ended Dr. Hocking's re-examination, but the Judge wanted to know if Stephen had died from inhaling vomit, whether an observer would have found some signs of vomit on the floor, or in the bed or on his person?

95

"Not by any means necessarily, my Lord," Dr. Hocking replied, "because at that time in the early morning most of the food he had at his late meal could have been digested. It only requires a small amount of vomit to go up the gullet and come down the air passage to cause a blockage, and it might not necessarily leave his mouth."

The Defence then called a second expert witness, Professor Arthur Mant, Professor of Forensic Medicine at the University of London.

He agreed that he had only been in Court that one day but had heard all Dr. Hocking's evidence. He had also had submitted to him all the material papers in the case. Professor Mant said that he accepted Dr. Hunt's findings of fact, but preferred the conclusions Dr. Hocking drew from them to those of Dr. Hunt.

The Professor was asked for his view on one of the Crown's theories, namely that the fracture of the rib some three to seven days before death might have been the direct cause of death through pneumonia supervening, owing to the rib having punctured the lung. Professor Mant pointed out that the fractured section of the rib was rounded, and that with that particular type of formation of bone at the end of the fracture it was unlikely to have punctured the lung. A sharper fragment would have been required. Stephen's movements about the house on the last evening of his life, as given in evidence by Elizabeth, also did not suggest that he was suffering from pneumonia. If he had pneumonia, he would probably not have been able to move about the house.

Professor Mant also discounted an alternative Crown theory, that the lung had not been pierced by the fracture three to seven days before death but had been penetrated by an assault on the night of Stephen's death. Even assuming, against his belief, that this had happened, the subsequent time schedule of events was all wrong.

"Is there anything to be said," asked Mr. Field-Fisher, "for what I understand to be the third possibility, that the boy's general health was so low, he was so debilitated, over a period of weeks and months leading up to the end, that the final assault was, as it were, the last straw and was sufficient to kill him?"

"I saw nothing in the committal statements that suggested he was debilitated," the Professor replied.

"You heard Dr. Hocking cross-examined about the pain that this boy must have suffered from the undoubted rib fractures over the preceeding weeks and months. What do you say about pain in relation to those sort of injuries and how it affects different people?"

"I saw nothing in the committal statements to suggest he had ever suffered pain," Professor Mant replied. "He had been to the dentist after some ribs had been fractured and there is no mention of him behaving abnormally. Some people have a very high pain threshold, and what may be very painful to you and me, may not cause them to suffer at all."

The professor accepted as a definite possibility Dr. Hocking's theory of the events which may have followed on from Stephen banging his head when falling over in his father's bedroom.

"Is it possible in this case," Counsel asked, "to give a definite cause of death?"

"No. In my opinion it is quite impossible."

"From the evidence that is available, what do you think is the likely possibility?"

"I would not like to speculate."

"Do you think that the whole thing is to some extent speculation?"

"Yes. We have got a decomposed body without cause of death."

"In your view, it is quite impossible to be sure one way or the other what the cause of death was?"

"Absolutely," Professor Mant replied.

Mr. Owen-Thomas rose to cross-examine the eminent Professor. Professor Mant agreed that he had had a relatively minor involvement in the case prior to trial. He had read the Depositions taken at the committal hearing on St. Mary's, he had examined the bones with Dr. Hunt at Plymouth on the 25th November, two weeks before the trial and wrote his report two days later.

"Professor Mant, you say there is nothing in the Depositions to show he suffered pain. Let us just think about it. Do you agree that when somebody has a fractured rib they will, to a greater or lesser extent, have a painful condition?"

"Pain or discomfort perhaps."

"Is it not going to be objectionable to have a broken rib?"

"It may be, yes." To the observer, it seemed strange that the professor could not make himself admit clearly and unambiguously, that a fractured rib would inevitably cause pain to the person concerned.

"Professor, if somebody has a broken rib which is untreated, every time he moves, if it is a complete severance, the ends are likely to rub together, are they not?"

"Yes."

"Are you saying that that is something which would not be objectionable to the sufferer?"

Professor Mant replied, "I have read through these Depositions and I can find no reference to pain from any witness. He apparently leads a perfectly normal life, he did the housework, he took the dogs for a walk, he went to the dentist and it was not noticed there. From that, I assume that he could not have suffered pain in the context that you put."

"Never mind about reading the Depositions. Just have a look at the box containing the ribs. Do you accept that that shows that this lad sustained fractures of the ribs?"

"Yes."

"On how many occasions do you say force was applied sufficient to cause those fractures?"

"Probably four times."

The Professor also agreed that the final fracture cracked inwards, and that the force generated by a rabbit punch would have been sufficient to cause that injury.

"If the rabbit punch were to land on an already virtually severed rib," Counsel asked, "not only would it be liable to separate the two ends completely, but it would also be capable of driving either one of those ends through the pleural cavity into the lung?"

"I think it is unlikely. It takes a lot to puncture a lung," replied Professor Mant.

"You just feel, if you will please, the ends of those two pieces of rib. They are sharp enough to be driven through the pleural cavity and into the lung, are they not?"

"I do not think so," came the response.

"If the rib did puncture the lung, do you agree," enquired Counsel, "that within two to twenty-four hours that lung would collapse?"

"Not necessarily," the Professor replied. "It depends entirely on the size of the tear. You can get the pleura penetrated and no immediate collapse and it usually repairs itself within a few hours, or you can get a deep laceration in which case the lung will collapse within a few minutes. That is my experience."

Mr. Owen-Thomas then asked, "If somebody is bleeding from the mouth, with blood trickling down the throat, and into the windpipe and down into the lung, that will also cause difficulty with breathing, will it not?"

"Yes."

"The victim then becomes starved of air, oxygen?"

"Yes."

"It is oxygen getting into the blood that keeps the brain functioning properly?"

"Yes."

"If someone is deprived of oxygen, their mental processes begin to work in a rather sluggish way?"

"Yes."

"Then they begin to become comatose and then can lose consciousness?"

"Yes."

"They can then in fact die?"

"Yes."

"That can happen from a rib puncturing a lung, can it not?"

"A deep puncturing of the lung, yes," Professor Mant replied.

Professor Mant said that he had come across one case, similar to

Stephen's, where a boy of nineteen fell down and hit his head against a radiator and died because of a haemorrhage from the artery at the base of the skull and blood leaked into the brain and killed him. Stephen, of course, did not have a haemorrhage of any size, but the Professor said that in Stephen's case he would not have expected to find any blood or staining because the blood "gets leached out in the earth and soil if the soil is wet." Neither would he have expected to find a fractured skull caused by Stephen's fall. He would, however, have expected "concussion followed by a lucid interval and then by increasing loss of consciousness."

Finally, Mr. Justice Willis asked Professor Mant a few questions: "Professor Mant, you have come here, being very experienced, as an expert witness in criminal matters, to give evidence. Do you feel any disadvantage at not having heard the evidence, except the cross-examination of Dr. Hocking?"

"No. I have read the statements."

"But you have not heard the evidence?"

"No, no, I have not heard the evidence."

"You know as well as I do," persisted the Judge, "that depositions or statements may differ from the evidence that has actually been given in the witness box?"

"From what I have heard here today, my Lord, I do not think I am under a disadvantage, because in my view, and it has been from the start, it is not possible to say what this young boy died of."

"There is no dispute about that," said the Judge.

"One could speculate," the Professor continued, "obviously as to the possible cause - natural, unnatural or accidental."

"Of course one can speculate all sorts of things if there is any evidence upon which to speculate, but are you really suggesting that there can be an accidental explanation of these injuries?" asked the Judge in amazement.

"I have heard some of the evidence today and I agree with some of it and I do not know from this evidence how his death came about," replied the Professor.

"Again," continued the Judge relentlessly, "you do not feel under any disadvantage in expressing the view you already have done to the Jury in not having heard the evidence of Dr. Hunt in examination and cross-examination?"

"I have seen a note of most of his evidence," came the reply.

DAY SEVEN

The next day of the trial, 14th December, saw the return to the witness box of Dr. Hunt. It is unusual for a prosecution witness to be recalled to give further evidence once the Defence have opened their case, but this is allowed with leave of the court where opinions are given by Defence experts which have not been dealt with by the corresponding Prosecution expert.

"Would you please take the box with the ribs in," asked Mr. Owen-Thomas. "You will remember that yesterday Professor Mant expressed the view that the fractured right rib, the seventh, was not sufficiently sharp to puncture the lung?"

"Yes," replied Dr. Hunt. "In my view this is sharp enough to go into the lung. But I am only saying this is a possibility. I do not think I could exclude it as much as Professor Mant does." He also confirmed his belief that a rabbit punch might cause the rib to enter the lung.

Two other defence witnesses, Mr. Gordon Brain, manager of the island Co-op where Stephen worked for six months in 1972, and Mr. Kenneth Williams, who used to help Menheniott with car repairs, both said they had never seen any signs of injury on Stephen. Both agreed under cross-examination, however, that they had never seen him other than fully clothed and would have been unable to see bruises on his body.

The remainder of the day was taken up with counsels closing speeches to the Jury, which dealt with the evidence, and the theories and possibilities which flowed from the evidence. Mr. Field-Fisher, very rightly, emphasised that it was the prosecution which had to prove its case, the defendant had to prove nothing, and that there could be no conviction of murder unless the Jury were sure that Menheniott intended to cause his son really serious, or grievous, bodily harm.

DAY EIGHT

Mr. Justice Willis commenced his summing-up on Thursday, 15th December. He asked the Jury to disregard anything they may have heard or read before the trial commenced, and emphasised that they should not be swayed by indignation at the unchallenged evidence of the long saga of ill-treatment meted out to Stephen and the manner of his burial.

"The facts are entirely a matter for you. I direct you on the law and you take the law from me. If I get it wrong, the Court of Appeal will put me right. I shall summarise the evidence. As will be apparent to all of you, a great deal of the evidence is common ground or not challenged. Therefore it would be wasting your time and an insult to your intelligence if I rehearsed in detail evidence to which you have listened so carefully.

"Your task here is not to decide what the cause of death was. Before there can be a conviction of murder you have got to be sure that Stephen died at the hands of the accused, whatever may have been the cause of death ultimately. That in a nutshell is what you have got to consider in this case.

"He faces, of course, very grave charges. Whether they are charges under count one, the charge of murder, or the hidden charge of manslaughter, or inflicting grievous bodily harm with intent to do so under counts three to six, they are all very grave charges under the criminal law. You will, of course, give them each your separate consideration. As a matter of convenience, it may be convenient for you to reach a decision on count one first, because if you convict the accused either of murder or manslaughter you will not be asked to give your verdict on counts three to six.

"The first count of murder consists of the unlawful killing of one person by another with intent to kill or do him really serious injury. The prosecution do not invite you to consider the question of an intention to kill. The evidence falls far short of that as a possible basis of that charge. What they do invite you to consider is whether you are sure that any injury inflicted on the boy, really on that last occasion, was inflicted with the intent to do injury to that extent.

"The prosecution case depends on inferences which you are invited to draw from the fractures which were found in four ribs, the dental history, together with the direct evidence of witnesses as to injuries caused by the accused prior to and including the day of death.

"If you feel sure that Stephen had been so weakened physically by continuous ill-treatment so that the violence which he received in the hall, if you accept Elizabeth's evidence, was the cause of his death a few hours later, that is, to use a neutral word at this point, homicide. Whether your verdict in a case of homicide is one of murder or manslaughter depends upon whether or not you feel sure that he intended at that time to do really serious injury.

"Members of the Jury, before there can be any conviction at all on count one, the Prosecution must exclude, first of all, natural causes as the cause of death and, secondly, accident, two matters which you have been invited to consider.

"You may feel that so far as natural causes are concerned, you can safely assume without very much further consideration that death did not take place due to natural causes. The question of accident has raised its head - a fall from a tree. What you may think at the end of the case must be a matter for you. The matter has been canvassed before you because, as you know, Elizabeth has told you that she was told by the accused to explain, I think, the tooth injury by a fall from the tree if anybody asked. You, no doubt, will have made up your minds by now whether you think that is a serious suggestion which you can take seriously, or whether you can safely dismiss from your minds any question of accident as a reasonable possibility in relation to any of the injuries."

It seems that at this stage the Jury were really only being asked by the Judge to consider accidental death in one context - that of the bump on the head in Menheniott's bedroom, which was the keystone of Dr. Hocking's theory as to the cause of death. The Jury could not convict of either murder or manslaughter unless they had first rejected Dr. Hocking's

101

theory with such support as he had received from Professor Mant.

"But you may feel that the circumstances are important on the question of whether the death may have been caused by an accidental bump on the head. There seems no doubt that he (Menheniott) spread around a story of Stephen's departure from the Island.... he wrote that fabricated letter to the same effect, and he lied consistently to the Police you may think with one purpose only, to try and put the Police off the scent. In this Court, he has admitted (by changing his plea to Guilty) that he disposed of that body in order to prevent the Coroner holding an Inquest. The Prosecution invite you to ask yourselves why. You may think that you should ask yourselves why.

"The accused has not gone into the witness box. He has declined to do so in the undoubted exercise of his right. You may think you have been deprived of an opportunity of hearing him tested in cross-examination."

Of Margaret Allwright's evidence (she was one of Menheniott's daughters and one year older than Stephen) the Judge said: "It is quite clear that Margaret dislikes her father, whether for good reason or not does not concern you. It is quite inevitable, having heard her evidence, that really very little reliance can be placed upon it."

The Judge then recapitulated in summary form some of the evidence of those Prosecution witnesses who had seen isolated acts of violence against Stephen between the years 1972, when he returned to the Islands, and 1975. He also summarised Mr. Fairest's evidence, and of the defence suggestion that Stephen's missing teeth had become dislodged one way or another in the grave, the Judge said: "The irresistible inference to be drawn is that there is no reasonable explanation for the teeth having been forced out after death in the grave, and Mr. Fairest's view of the matter, that that had been done by two blows shortly before death, is an explanation which you may find acceptable."

After outlining Elizabeth Rayner's evidence in detail, including the various assaults she witnessed, the leg bandaging session and her subsequent visit to Stephen's bedroom, the Judge said: "No one has suggested that Elizabeth is lying. The reason that I have reminded you in detail about her evidence is because you may feel that in all the circumstances hers is evidence that does not receive some confirmation from elsewhere and requires your very careful consideration. That, of course, applies whether it is evidence which is relied upon by the Prosecution or by the Defence."

The Judge then dealt with the rival theories of the Pathologists, although he seemed to discount Professor Mant's testimony as he had not heard the evidence but had merely relied on the written committal statements. Dr. Hocking, he said, disagreed with Dr. Hunt's opinions because of Elizabeth's testimony that Stephen was in perfectly normal health up to the time that he had his legs bandaged in his father's bedroom on the night of his death. Dr. Hunt's theories really discounted such a possibility, since in his opinion Stephen would have been very ill by his last day. Was Stephen exhibiting normal behaviour that evening, asked the Judge? Was Elizabeth's recollection correct - she had after all suffered a severe stroke since that fateful evening? "It is," said the Judge, "a matter entirely for you. Because it is your decision whether you accept Elizabeth's evidence as sufficient for (Dr. Hocking's) theory.

"If you prefer the views of Dr. Hocking to those of Dr. Hunt, and you think that his explanation may reasonably be the correct one as to the cause of death, then, of course you will acquit the accused of murder or manslaughter. If you think, on the other hand, that the basis for Dr. Hocking's opinion is not sufficiently reliable, and you do not accept the description that Elizabeth gives as being one from which it would be reasonable to infer that he was behaving normally and was in normal health, then, of course, there is no basis left for Dr. Hocking's theory."

Of the Police evidence, as outlined earlier, the Judge said: "That is evidence which from the beginning to the end of the record is unchallenged. You have got to decide whether the account of these interviews with the Police assists you in the decision to which you have got to come. That he lied and invented of course, cannot be denied. Of course, that he lied and lied again does not necessarily mean that he is guilty of any offence. But it is a factor in this story to which you are entitled to attach such weight as you think right."

The day's proceedings then closed with Mr. Justice Willis indicating that he would complete his summing-up the next morning, Friday, 16th December.

DAY NINE

"Members of the Jury, I had concluded last night all I wanted to say to you by way of summing-up. All I want to say to you now is that when you retire, will you try to reach verdicts upon which you are all agreed, unanimous verdicts. Do not worry your heads about majority verdicts at this stage. If you are unable to reach unanimous verdicts then I shall give you a further direction. I will ask you now not to think of majority verdicts. Will you try to reach unanimous verdicts?"

The law as to acceptance by the court of a majority verdict is laid down in the Juries Act, 1974. The first stipulation is that the majority must be at least ten. Secondly, the court cannot accept a majority verdict unless the jury have had such period of time for deliberation as the court thinks reasonable, having regard to the nature and complexity of the case; and the court shall in any event not accept such a verdict unless the jury have had at least two hours for deliberation.

******

The Jury retired to consider their verdict at 10.36 a.m. Their first duty would have been to select a Foreman, who would chair their deliberations.

******

The hours passed until eventually at 2.15 p.m. the Jury returned to court.

The Clerk of the Court: "Will the Foreman stand, please? Will you answer my first question 'Yes' or 'No'. Have the Jury reached a verdict upon which they are all agreed?"

"No," replied the Foreman.

Mr. Justice Willis: "Mr. Foreman, you have now been deliberating, I think, about three and a half hours, and therefore I think it appropriate to give you a direction with regard to majority verdicts. I am going to ask you to retire again, and ask you, if you can, to reach a unanimous verdict. If you are unable to do that I shall be able to accept a verdict on which no less than ten of you are agreed. Will you retire again."

****

The Jury retired again at 2.17 p.m. and returned to court at 2.34 p.m. Menheniott, black-bearded and powerfully built, stood unmoved and expressionless as the Jury of ten men and two women, through their Foreman, prepared to announce their verdict.

The Clerk: "Will the Foreman stand, please. Mr. Foreman, please answer this question 'Yes' or 'No'. Have at least ten of you agreed upon your verdict?"

The Foreman: "Yes."

"On the first count of the Indictment, do you find William Thomas Menheniott Guilty or Not Guilty of Murder?"

"Guilty."

"Is that the verdict of you all, or by a majority?"

"By a majority."

"How many of you agreed upon that verdict and how many dissented?"

"Eleven for, and one against."

****

Mr. Justice Willis then discharged the Jury from giving verdicts on the remaining counts on the indictment and said they would remain on the file. He then gaoled farm worker Menheniott for life on the murder charge and also gave him a concurrent sentence of five years imprisonment for burying Stephen's body in order to avoid a coroner's inquest. Menheniott, after nine days in the dock, showed no sign of emotion as prison warders led him away to the cells.

Menheniott's departure to the cells was not, however, the end of this tragic saga. It had become clear during the course of the trial that various questions outside the jurisdiction of the criminal courts required answering. The main question that required an answer was how had Stephen, a simple lad in the care of East Sussex County Council, been allowed to return to his father at Holy Vale in August, 1972 at the age of fifteen, when it was abundantly evident that Menheniott was a totally unsuitable person to oversee his future well-being? It seemed that the Judge must have given Counsel an indication of his concern some time before the Jury returned with their verdict, as the relevant Authorities were legally represented when the Judge made his concluding remarks in open court.

He said there was a large question mark which had been hanging over the case for a long time and which he wished to discuss with Counsel on both sides in public. It was, he said, a matter which must still be exercising the minds of the general public "as it is exercising mine." How had it come about that, with one single exception, so far as he knew "not a single soul in that community in three years seems to have done a thing to help that boy, who was obviously in fear of his father, as has been deposed to by a number of witnesses who have been called in this case?"

The single exception, said the Judge, was Mr. Fairest, the St. Mary's dental surgeon, who was obviously exceedingly worried about Stephen's condition in the autumn of 1975, but who was subject to considerable difficulties because of the constraints imposed upon him by his professional position.

"The boy must have been showing signs, that were painfully obvious, of injuries of one sort and another, and which I should have thought would have been obvious to anybody who was not either anxious to turn a blind eye or who possibly went in fear of the reactions of the accused."

That was a matter that affected only the members of the small community of the island of St. Mary's. "But there is another matter too," said the Judge. "If ever there was a problem family, it seems to me it was the Menheniotts. They have been known for years to one local authority after another and the problems were notorious. Yet this boy came at the end of 1972 from the care of the East Sussex County Council, and although it is no part of my duty to hold any sort of inquiry, I would be failing in my public duty if I did not express my own concern about what happened.

"I want to know what steps were taken either by the East Sussex County Council or by the Cornwall County Council, or both, to see how the boy fared in his new habitat."

Mr. Owen-Thomas, Q.C., said he had asked the Director of Social Services for Cornwall, Mr. Neil McLellan, about this, and it appeared that when East Sussex mooted the idea that Stephen should go home to live, the

Cornwall County Council's Social Services Department had been against the idea. They had said he should not be returned home and they refused to accept responsibility for Stephen being 'thrust towards them.' They made it plain that they did not think it right.

Mr. David Davies, a barrister instructed by the East Sussex County Council, then gave a resumé of Stephen's life in their care, and continued: "The time came when he was due to leave school at the age of sixteen and the County Council found themselves in a grave dilemma. He had not developed greatly in care and they had been unable to find work or a home for him in the long term. In those circumstances, and also because he wanted to go back to the Scilly Isles, they sent him back although he was still in their care until he was eighteen."

Mr. Justice Willis, interrupting, said: "So that over the whole of the period of those terrible three years - he reached his eighteenth birthday in June, 1975 - he was in the care of the East Sussex County Council? For the greater part of that time they were the authority exercising parental responsibilities, or rather not exercising them."

Mr. Davies replied: "There was no transference of parental responsibility, but the Scilly Isles were told that he was going back. What they said, and I mention this in no way as a criticism, was that they would do what they could to keep an eye on the situation and if problems came to light they would let East Sussex know."

Mr. Davies said that in practise the Scillies relied for advice on the County of Cornwall, which had made its position clear. "I am not endeavouring to set up any kind of strife between the authorities and it is right to say that parental responsibility remained with East Sussex."

"So the fact of the matter," said the Judge, "is that from the day this boy set foot in the Scilly Isles in 1972, there was no visiting, monitoring, I think the jargon is, by any of these three authorities?"

"There were no visits by East Sussex or by Cornwall," Mr. Davies replied.

Mr. McLellan, Director of Social Services for Cornwall, then went into the witness box and told the Judge that the Cornwall County Council was involved in Stephen's supervision with East Sussex in 1968 and 1969 while Stephen was on the Island. "Then he went back to Sussex and from that point on we had no direct dealing whatever with his care. We did offer some views to East Sussex when the question of the possibility of him coming back to the islands was being considered, but we recognised that the decisions concerning Stephen's future care and supervision rested with them."

Mr. Justice Willis then asked: "So the East Sussex County Council knew that if they sent this boy back, the Cornwall County Council washed their hands of him as a supervising authority?"

"I would not like to use the phrase that we were prepared to wash

106

our hands of it," protested Mr. McLellan.

"But you were not prepared to do anything about it," pressed the Judge. "You were not prepared to take him under your supervision?" "That is so," replied Mr. McLellan.

Mr. Davies, on behalf of East Sussex, said that a lot had happened since 1972, and procedures that now existed, although it was no consolation to Stephen, would have prevented such a lack of supervision occuring.

The Judge said he regarded all he had heard as gravely disturbing and said he proposed to communicate with the responsible Governmental Department about the case.

"To conclude the proceedings of this tragic case on a rather different note, I want to express my admiration, which I am sure the Jury and Counsel share, for the work which has been done by Superintendent Dennis Lovell and his Police team to unravel the mystery of the boy's disappearance and to bring his father to justice. They deserve the thanks of the public for what they have done."

Chapter 6

Repercussions

With the Judge's remonstrations ringing in everyone's ears, the judicial proceedings at Bodmin were thus brought to an end. The Islanders of St. Mary's were indeed shaken by the Judge's strictures. Perhaps it was that those who had seen violence inflicted upon Stephen over the years did not wish to be thought of as 'busybodies' and perhaps also they thought, and hoped, that the incidents they had witnessed were isolated ones? Certainly an indictment of the whole island community would be totally unjust, as it was only a very small number of residents who ever witnessed violence, and then only in the form of isolated incidents. For instance, Mrs. Hicks, the riding instructor, passed Holy Vale many times, but only saw one incident.

Until April, 1975, the islanders had resisted the appointment of a professional social worker, believing there was insufficient work. Mrs. Maureen Wooley was then appointed as a part-time social worker, but she resigned in January, 1977 and no new appointment was made. Mrs. Woolley was never asked to visit the Menheniotts, but she says that she would have consulted the Cornwall Social Services Officers if anything concerning Stephen had been referred to her. Even though Cornwall had never accepted any responsibilities towards Stephen upon his return to the islands in 1972, it does seem strange that the county never arranged for any of its social services officers to make occasional informal visits. They must surely have suspected that East Sussex were doing nothing.

It is not surprising, in the light of the remarks made by Mr. Justice Willis at the conclusion of the trial, that within a month a decision had been taken to initiate an Inquiry. In response to a demand from Mr. Robert Hicks, M.P. for Bodmin, Mr. David Ennals, Secretary of State for Social Services, decided that an Inquiry into the case of Stephen Menheniott would be set up and that the ensuing report would be published.

In the meantime, however, Menheniott had been advised to appeal against his conviction of murder. His application for leave to appeal was heard by the Court of Appeal at the Royal Courts of Justice in London on 5th February, 1979 before the Lord Chief Justice, Lord Widgery, sitting with Lord Justice Eveleigh and Mr. Justice Stephen Brown. Mr. Field-Fisher, Q.C. again appeared for Menheniott and Mr. Owen-Thomas for the Crown.

After hearing legal argument, the Lord Chief Justice delivered the Court's decision. He outlined the facts of the case as established by the evidence, and continued: "The Prosecution case was that the victim had undoubtedly died at his father's hands. At the end of the day there can, we think, be no doubt about the correctness and truth of that assertion. There remained, however, two possible alternatives: one, that he died as a result of an accidental injury, namely the injury he suffered when he slipped in his father's bedroom and fell and, as the alternative, there was a possibility that he died as a result of his father's more direct activities in the form of the various blows which must have given rise to the injuries suffered.

"The Crown theory, put more precisely, was simply this: the boy seemed to have a high threshold of pain, which perhaps will explain some of the failures to complain, but the Crown contended there was a perfectly cogent explanation of his death on which they could rely. The cogent explanation was that Stephen, in various ways and as a result of continuous maltreatment, had become much debilitated and was open to attack of viruses and the like, and that the happenings in the father's cottage on the last night, which I have described were, as it were, the last straw on a body already damaged by broken ribs and such injuries of that kind.

"The main contention of the Defence was that the Prosecution must fail because it could not positively prove the cause of death. At the trial, the Court was invited to conclude that the story told by the Defence, supported by Elizabeth Rayner, that there had been an accidental slip and fall, was itself a coherent explanation of what had occured.

"If we thought for a moment this was a case in which the cause of death could not be ascertained we should, of course, allow the appeal because proof of the cause of death would be vital in a matter such as this.

"But it does not seem to us there is any handicap on the Crown in this regard. There is an explanation, as given by Dr. Hunt, which is acceptable in the sense that it is cogent and not in any way overridden by the other evidence and which it was proper to leave to the Jury so that the Jury could consider it side by side with the alternative version, namely the death by accident version which the defence were seeking to run. It seems to us that once we reach the point of being able to say the Judge was right to leave this issue to the Jury, there is no more to be said about the case because the Jury unquestionably took the view that this was a case of murder, and apart from one or two very minor matters there is no criticism of the summing-up upon which they considered their verdict.

"Despite the considerable effort and the considerable time which this uphappy affair has occupied in the past, it seems to us that at this, the final stage, we can deal with it with comparative brevity. We will sum up our views by saying in regard to the theories submitted by both the Crown and the Defence, they have been tenable theories properly left to the Jury and we are satisfied the Jury accepted one of those theories. The end result," said the Lord Chief Justice in conclusion, "is we do not consider this conviction unsafe or unsatisfactory in any degree. The application for leave to appeal is therefore refused."

Thus ended the judicial process, but one was still left to ponder how such horrific and scandalous events could possibly have come about? The relevant events witnessed had been spread over a period from August 1972 to January 1976. The islanders are caring people, and the explanation why no-one reported matters to the Authorities can be explained by the fact that no single Islander had ever witnessed sustained violence. The only exception to this was Elizabeth Rayner, but she, owing to her rather ambivalent role in the home, was clearly completely under the control of, and subservient to, her father, and to that extent was not truly a free agent. With hindsight, no doubt, every islander who gave evidence was wishing that events they had witnessed had been reported to the authorities, but life's passage would be so easy with the benefit of hindsight and violent death often easier to avoid.

There were, however, two fundamental questions that still remained unanswered. First, why did East Sussex return Stephen to his father in 1972 at the age of 15, when they knew of his totally unsatisfactory character and when such a decision went against the express wishes of the Cornish authorities? And secondly, once Stephen had returned to St. Mary's in 1972, why did East Sussex totally fail to supervise his progress and welfare?

It was basically to answer these two questions, that between the end of Menheniott's trial in 1977 and his appeal in 1979 the Secretary of State for Social Services requested the Department of Health and Social Security to conduct an investigation into the background to the case. Their Report was in due course published by H.M.S.O. under the title 'Report of the Social Work Service of D.H.S. into certain aspects of the management of the case of Stephen Menheniott.'

In connection with these two questions, the Report concluded: "We consider that those who took the decision to allow him to stay at home in 1972 placed too great an emphasis on Stephen's own wishes by contrast with the weight given to the opinion of officers in the East Sussex assessment centre, and in Cornwall, who had close knowledge of him and his family. Insufficient consideration appears to have been given to alternative solutions. The decision to allow Stephen to remain at home having been made, the failure to discuss with Cornwall their refusal to supervise, or to visit him, or to review his case, is indefensible, as was the closure of the case before he reached the age of eighteen. No officer of East Sussex has attempted to defend these omissions."

The Report also stated: "The question may also be raised as to why since supervision had been provided willingly in 1968/9, the Children's Officer for Cornwall took such a decisive stand against offering it, even under informal arrangements, when Stephen returned home in 1972. Her explanation was that after the incest case, and Stephen's mother's departure from the family, circumstances had changed to such an extent as to make effective supervision impossible. This explanation was apparently

110

accepted by East Sussex. They did not question it and they made no further request for help from Cornwall. There is in any case no legal requirement on any authority to undertake supervision on behalf of another authority."

Whilst East Sussex cannot escape censure for their part in this unhappy saga, it is true to say that no complaints of ill-treatment by Menheniott towards his son were ever made to any of the relevant authorities, and it cannot be denied that great difficulties face local authorities when endeavouring to carry out parental responsibilities. In some cases parental links have to be severed completely, whilst in others the child in care may be allowed to live with his parents. The decision can often be difficult and heartrending and it is inevitable that sometimes mistakes will be made, and often when a decision is taken there is an acknowledged element of risk involved. In a case such as Stephen's, question after question can be asked: why did not East Sussex take up with Cornwall their refusal to assist in supervision? Why did not East Sussex visit Stephen at Holy Vale? If Menheniott had refused supervisory visits, why was Stephen not removed from home? Why did not East Sussex register Stephen with a doctor? Why did East Sussex discharge Stephen from their care on 9th December, 1974 when he was only seventeen-and-a-half?

At the end of the day, however, it has to be accepted that all the evidence suggests that Stephen would inevitably have decided to return to his father when East Sussex's parental rights automatically terminated on 4th June, 1975, his eighteenth birthday. Perhaps the final question that should be posed, therefore, is whether on that assumption, Stephen would have avoided the ill-treatment which, in the event, led him to the shallow grave in California Field? Clearly he should have been given the chance.

111